D1569146

LIFEFORM

Also by Jenny Slate

Marcel the Shell with Shoes On: Things About Me
(with Dean Fleischer-Camp)

Marcel the Shell: The Most Surprised I've Ever Been
(with Dean Fleischer-Camp)

Little Weirds

Jenny Slate

Little, Brown and Company
New York Boston London

Little, Brown and Company
Hachette Book Group
1290 Avenue of the Americas, New York, NY 10104
littlebrown.com

First Edition: October 2024

Little, Brown and Company is a division of Hachette Book Group, Inc. The Little, Brown name and logo are trademarks of Hachette Book Group, Inc.

The publisher is not responsible for websites (or their content) that are not owned by the publisher.

The Hachette Speakers Bureau provides a wide range of authors for speaking events. To find out more, go to hachettespeakersbureau.com or call (866) 376-6591.

Little, Brown and Company books may be purchased in bulk for business, educational, or promotional use. For information, please contact your local bookseller or the Hachette Book Group Special Markets Department at special.markets@hbgusa.com.

Excerpt from *The Hearing Trumpet* copyright © 1974, 2021 by Leonora Carrington, used by permission of New York Review Books.

ISBN 9780316263931 (hardcover) / 9780316583466 (B&N.com signed edition) / 9780316586870 (signed edition)
LCCN 2024939461

Printing 1, 2024

LSC-C

Printed in the United States of America

For Ben and Ida

For my family

Here I may add that I consider that I am still a useful member of society and I believe still capable of being pleasant and amusing when the occasion seems fit. The fact that I have no teeth and never could wear dentures does not in any way discomfort me, I don't have to bite anybody.

—Leonora Carrington, *The Hearing Trumpet*

Contents

Contents

Phase 3: Pregnancy

Phase 4: Baby

Contents

Phase 5: Ongoing

LIFEFORM

Letters to the Doctor: Stonehenge

Dear Doctor,

I hope that you had a delicious Thanksgiving.

Doctor, I have been to Stonehenge. Maybe you can tell by my blood sample?

When I was sixteen years old, I went to England to participate in a summer program at Oxford University. To me, it seemed that I was basically going to college, and what lent credibility to this feeling was that I had recently gotten the metal braces off my teeth, after seven years of metal braces affixed to each tooth, with the wires and elastics as well. I had turned sixteen that spring, and my grandmother had taken me to a department store to get my first supply of makeup, and I had started to menstruate shortly thereafter. It seemed to me that a chain reaction was under way, the "real deal" had begun, and it might even be possible to experience my first kiss. As this sixteen-year-old, I dressed myself in clothes that I now know would be called "business casual," because I wrongly thought they were similar to clothes that women wore when they were the main character of a TV show about people dating and having a career in a city.

During the monthlong summer program at Oxford University, we went on many excursions, including a day trip to Stonehenge. I went there on a bus, wearing pearl earrings in my earlobes and a huge pad in my underpants. I took about eleven pictures of Stonehenge with my disposable camera.

Recently, I found a box of photographs that I took throughout the 1990s, and they were all out of order. The box of photographs was from my childhood home, which had recently been sold, and in what felt like a huge rush, my family was expunged from the place. It felt more like a shipwreck than an intentional move. When I opened the box, I sensed a secondary, personal shipwreck straggling ashore. There was a remote part of me that wanted to scan the floorboards to make sure that they were not wet by some sort of flat, salty wash. The photos showed a lot of faces that I remembered, but I could not put names to many of those faces. It was fairly straining to discover that I had recorded so much and that it was now worthless to me. Mostly, this random box made me feel as if my entire life has an unfindable leak, and most of the photos allowed for me to feel nothing but this feeling of the unfindable leak, but when I came upon the pictures of Stonehenge, I thought, "There they are! The stones!"

Nobody really knows what went on there at Stonehenge. That is the best part about it. It is a huge mystery and the stones are just sitting there in a field and anyone can go, and for some reason no jokers have come around to do spray paint on them. It was the Druids, they say. Well, okay? And my boyfriend and I watched a presentation on the computer about how they got the stones over there, but it did not solve it for me. I still felt the hunger that you feel with living mysteries.

So here is where we get to why I am writing to you today, Doctor. Have you any experience with patients who suddenly understood something, and then even though they had other things to do, they could not stop fixating on that new understanding? I guess the question is: How many patients of yours are affected by arresting revelations? Like the revelation itself is saying, *Keep thinking about me, there is more, don't let go of me, keep digging?* Is this a common occurrence? Please keep this confidential—do not even use me anonymously for a case study in a presentation, please. What I understood, sitting on the rug and looking at these pictures taken by my sixteen-year-old self who was outfitted with a small plank of bloody gauze in her underwear, was that *Stonehenge, these huge silenced rocks from long ago, is Witches That Got Turned into Rocks.*

The strange thing about the stones is how they are just there in the field, and even though they are stones, you feel that *they feel* that they are cold. First it started as me looking at the photographs and being like, "Oh, okay, are these rocks that only Witches could *lift*?" And then I was paralyzed, holding this picture of old stones, a picture from a box from my home that I could not return to, and I heard and saw in my mind: *The rocks are waiting for a storm, a wise, hot, and formidable storm that will only arrive when it knows the time has come. The rocks are waiting for this storm to come and float them up into the eye of itself, and then the stones will be cleaned with hot rain until they are made warm again. And then, obviously, when the warmth seeps far enough into the rocks, they will crack open and let their Witches out.* And there would probably be a buttload of lightning at that point too, Doctor.

And sadly one of the Witches will be stone-gray and actually dead. But then—wait! She is in fact a velvety gray bird with ebony legs, and she is actually the special one in the group! But she still cannot talk, she lost that. She can only do bird noises, so the other Witches are always like, "What did you say, Ogma?" And then she will give a look or a marble-y sound and they will understand her in their souls.

The Witches do not soak in the storm for very long, only long enough to wake up, get washed and warmed, and reaffirm their purpose. Then they come back down here to do big work, but within small stories. They get to work right away.

They find that theirs is very refreshing work, because there are so many sweethearts all over! Whenever it happened that the Druids or something else (maybe even the Witches themselves?) cast the Witches into the stones, there were fewer people on the planet. Now each Witch is thrilled to have so much to work with. They perform small acts, constantly. They are listeners and listen without ever stopping. They listen up for people saying *thank you* to strangers and send them great ideas, good dreams, or general good fortune that runs on its own. They start killing all the ticks and scabies, they remind kind older people that they can still have best friends, they make flights and flights of airplanes safe, they fill stomachs, pair animals and humans, suck away bitterness, cut tension, shrink all of the bad tumors, flick pain away, spread coin around. They touch the evening right on the sky and make it romantic or significant, and many people feel that they are encountering the auspicious, and they are. They bump up all the gardens, any vine with a grape or flower or gourd. There are so many new, lovely singers. They bless every single doorway, they turn all of the guns into brooms, they shatter the internet, and they put it into the mind of every baby that every other baby is their beloved. And this is just some of it.

They waited too long in their stones. They are not in a rush or a worry, but they cannot help but make up for lost time. Doctor, one day I know that people will go from being like, "What actually *is* Stonehenge?" to being like, "Why did the Witches have to wait so long in their rocks? What delayed the storm?"

What I am saying, Doctor, is that when I was sixteen, I took eleven pictures of these stones, set up in their field, waiting to be taken in, made ready, and released. *Now* I know what is in the picture, but I did not know when I took it, yet something in me still pushed me to record it.

I guess my question is, knowing you have my blood and pictures of my skeleton, is there any chance that I too have been out cold in a standing stone for a long time? I ask this because I feel a kinship to the stones and what I now understand about the Witches, and the work that they do. I ask because even though I have all of these pictures and they are evidence of my living, there is a lot of my life that seems like it happened while I was stuck inside of something.

How many patients have you been able to properly diagnose as "Stone Sleepers," which I understand to be a variety of Witch? You know me—I can just keep going as I am. I can just keep feeling my way along and let it rip every now and then, but I do feel that if I could be officially diagnosed, it would be like a warm washing, an essential ceremony to officially get me up and running, and then I would be able to relax into what I am. It would be like telling a Lion that they are a Lion, so then when they roar and when they hunt, they know that it is natural and that it is their big work and it would be really weird for them to *not* be doing it.

And the thing that makes the wish for a diagnosis a bit urgent, Doctor, is that the people who bought my family's house (the house where the box of pictures had been for so long) are two brothers who said that they were buying it for their own elderly parents. What a kind act! The house is an old colonial with large windows and a large, wide front porch and amber-glass doorknobs on all doors. We know for a fact that Georgia O'Keeffe once spent the night there, because the first owners were her cousins, the O'Keeffes. What a nice present these brothers purchased for their parents! That famous artist might have even dreamed of one of those clit-flower paintings in that very home!

But then when the papers were signed, it turned out that the brothers were nothing but liars, because it turned out that the house was not a present for their parents (who live in Florida and are not coming north), but that these brothers were going to knock it down to do pricey real estate development on its spot. Making deals, Doctor—they could feel it right in their penises, the deal that they could make by lying to my parents about their own parents. My parents would have had second thoughts about selling to them if they had been told the truth of what was to come. My bet is that either these brothers were proud of the swindle or they didn't notice it as anything but business as usual. My bet is also that they are not aware of the artwork of Georgia O'Keeffe.

This was already hard enough to take, the lying about their parents, but still, I tried to be mature about it in an effort to get what I wanted. I did not want a fight—after all, I am an adult and who cares about my childhood home? I am fortunate to have ever lived there at all, and I know that, Doctor. I just wanted some of the doorknobs and a small stained-glass window from the house. I wanted one of the basement stairs, the plank of wood that lay beneath the part of the ceiling that hung low. It has a white duck painted on a maroon background, and that was to remind you to *duck* down. I wanted to rescue these things from the specific type of disrespect that is obliteration, so I asked to be put in contact with one of the brothers so that I could buy back some of these items. I was shocked to find out that he was younger than I am. I had assumed he was old and faithless, not young and shitty. He wrote back a corporate-toned email about how they were "not ready to make any changes yet," and so I wrote back to say that I would like to come and take the items and buy them before they destroy the home, and I made sure to say "destroy the home," just in case he was actually alive in his heart. But I would love to do a bit more work in that area of trying to help him to see the effect he has on people, of making contact with what might be alive in his heart, I suppose.

I'm not saying I would do what the Witches would do; after all, they have been at this a really long time. Like, for example, the Witches would almost certainly send him dry fungus patches on his skin, all over, little almond-shaped gray patches with itches that never stop. Then, of course, if he ever slept through the itching, the Witches would touch his dreams: visions of his bloated hand slammed in a car door, recurring dreams of a constant drip of yellow from his butthole, stained pants and yellow down the leg. And every morning right before waking, he would dream a flock of sheep with teeth of pewter, advancing on his home, and he would know that they want to eat his physical ass with their dull, blunt old-metal teeth. Like a true loser, he would wake holding his butt cheeks together because he does not want his crack to get ripped into by dream-sheep.

That's what the Witches would do. But as for me, maybe I would just write a piece about him and put it in a book, for example, just say the truth about how I feel about how he does his business on earth. I would start small, like maybe working out my rage through an outrageous fantasy, one that allows for my fury but also leaves room for mercy, and titillates me a little bit. In the years before, I would have said nothing and I would have told myself that somehow this loss and this situation of being lied to had something to do with my own low worth, something to do with an unfindable leak in myself or my life, an unfindable leak that drains me of my power. But I am different now. I don't think that I brought this on. And I do have a response.

You can be asleep in a stone for so long, and so much can happen without your consent, and so much can happen because you are awake in the stone but afraid to even make a peep. But once you are out, once you get busted out, you can work freely and make up for lost time. You can respond. When I review my new understanding concerning the photos, the rocks, the Witches, and even the brothers who bought my family's house, it is not simply that I understand what power has been slumbering inside. It is that I realize that *of course* I have the power to punish, but this is only a small trick compared to what I am capable of. Doctor, I have weathered my own hot storm. And it is not just that I have been washed; it is that I have been warmed. I do not wish to live forever in the poisonous fantasy where I punish perfectly and perpetually. I do not want to be as cold as a stone and dirty with what splatters back at me from my own combat. I want to be as warm as a live person and I want to be clean enough to be around the very young or the very vulnerable. I want to live in reality and spin my rage into something new, edible.

I think that the storm came down and woke me up because it knew that I finally wanted more than to sit and stew and bitterly snarl about what I find to be "bad." I believe that my storm came when it knew that I wanted to be free and that I was ready to do my new work. The new work is to be able to forgive not just the ones who hurt or frightened or trapped me, but of course, it is the slow work of forgiving all of the specters inside of me who still spit, "Why were you even around those stones in the first place?" and "Why didn't you bust out earlier?" One by one, I must forgive the shames and cruelties I have slung at myself for choices made at desperate moments, or for spending so long waiting for literally anyone but myself to tell me that I am indeed the creature that I suspect I am. This is the only debt I have to pay, forgiveness by forgiveness until I have brought myself far from any spooky stones and foggy fields and I am in my own arms again. I can see clearly now that my strength has just begun to flow and that I am about to fledge.

Doctor, obviously I am sold on this diagnosis of "Stone Sleeper Witch," but please let me know if there is a test I should take, like the one I did for the ADHD. I think the medicine works but you can probably tell from this letter that nothing can really tame the wind, so to speak.

Kindly, with kindness,

J

Phase 1: Single

Light Bites

Five years ago I was finishing writing a book and I'd gone to my parents' house on an island so that I could be totally alone and hopefully more focused, and not just jumping out of desk and dining room chairs and then running away from my work to do a fake task that "I just remembered I need to do!" And one day in the middle of a morning during this trip, I decided, *Why not drive to the diner on the other end of the island and have something there?* I had not thought of what. I did have some things to eat in the house, but I thought maybe I would just take the drive and then have a light bite over there. I suppose I was still breaking the rules of focusing-up, but it felt a bit different because I did have to have a meal at some point. It is maybe sad to say, but when I am alone, I find it hard to have full meals, and I do not really know how to "cook for one," so when I am single I often have "light bites" at different intervals before the sun sets, like the elderly do. I like the elderly and I like eating this way, so actually it is not very sad, in my view. I drove the length of the island and got myself to the diner. I was seated in one of those good booths that are just for one person. It is a booth for one but it *could* be for two, which is low-pressure but also hopeful.

There was an elderly couple in one of the normal booths that are built to hold up to four people. The elderly man was talking in a loud horn of a voice and saying to the elderly woman, "I DON'T KNOW WHY IT'S SO HARD TO UNDERSTAND!" and she said, "Because it's *your head* thinking it!" And then he wanted to leave but she wanted to finish her soft drink, and I took notice of them and thought, in my single booth, *I never want that to happen to me.*

But then they were laughing and I thought, *I want that.*

Unfortunately, I have always believed that if there was something unlikable about me that would become apparent, the *likable* qualities about me would be instantly erased, and then the relationship would probably end. This led to trying to be *only likable*, which of course caused me to feel very angry and resentful toward the person I was trying to impress, and then I would feel *so* put upon for being "forced to be perfect" and I would forget that I was the one who had started it, I was doing the forcing! And then to myself I would seem *so unlikable*, which would lead to me telling myself that I *was* very unlikable and therefore my partner would soon bust me on this unlikability and then dump me for it. And then I would have really hurt my own feelings and I would say to myself, "Okay, I do not want to be with you anymore, Jenny." And then usually very soon after that, the other person would say it to me as well, and then I *would* be with myself, which was not what I'd wanted.

The old lady turned around to the booth behind her and asked two other elders what they had there at their table. One woman said "clam chowder," the other woman said that "Arlene got a hot dog and fries," but she did not say what she herself was having. When I overheard this, I thought, *There is a lot of neutral information out there as well.* And this was very calming. I was unsure about who Arlene was, but that was fine and not a stressor for me. I never heard what the second lady was having for lunch, and it was nice for me to experience letting go, just realizing that it was fine that I did not find out that information. The picture was still complete in its own way.

I also loved that it seemed like all of the customers knew each other. I appeared to be the only "rando" and I was wondering how many times I should come here so that the people would start to notice me and wonder about who I am, just an overall "There's that random woman again—what's her story?" How many times could I come to the diner until I could introduce myself to the hostess because she sees me so often, and then she would know my name? When I would come in after that point in time, I could say, "Hi, Lisa," and have it feel wonderfully luxurious because I really wanted it to happen that she knew me and that we both firmly understood that I was a "regular." It would feel luxurious, but also totally plausible, like how it felt to have an engagement ring when I had one before.

Scanning around a bit, I realized that most people in the restaurant were old, which was nice for me because I often feel my happiest when I am surrounded by the elderly, but this was a lot of old people. The wish for old people seemed to have bloomed too heavy for the stalk. And everyone was worrying about the bathroom key. I had a brief moment of panic where I jarred myself by wondering if I was actually in a dream, but it passed in a flash and I was steady again and doing my eaves-dropping that I love to do.

I heard the same lady who had clam chowder say to the lady in the couple, "We were at the hairdresser's, that's why." How lovely, really, just that story: She and someone (Arlene? Doesn't matter) were at the hairdresser's, and then they came here to have a light bite of lunch, and she had clam chowder and Arlene got a hot dog and this other lady had *who cares/it's fine.*

I had a BLT and coffee, just a light bite, just like all the others here at luncheon.

At that point in my life, the issue of finding a partner felt like one that never ceased, it was grinding away 24/7, it never rested and never allowed rest for me either. The trip to the diner offered a good alternative to me. To be in the diner with all of the elderly retired people who were just getting their hair shaped and eating clams and hot dogs and being in relationship to each other and going to the bathroom, it just all felt more like a "Here I am" and this meant nothing more or nothing less, and it was such a huge relief to not see a problem, but also not be lying about my life by refusing to acknowledge a problem. Everything in my life was still the same, and yet there was not a problem now, no problem at all.

A honker might need to blare it into your head, but no matter how you come to realize it, "it's *your head* thinking it" is actually the key to what you are experiencing. But you do have to identify the key. Everything felt so much easier to me then—not that I had given up on finding a companion, not even that I cared less about that pursuit, but that I did not have to stress out because of an absence. I felt able to totally unwind, and my life felt refurbished by a perspective that was very easy to understand. I saw what was real, and I was a part of it. I was enjoying a simple meal in a gentle context that allowed me to rest a bit while still asking for and receiving things from the world at large. There was a time when eating alone in a restaurant would have caused me to do a rude inventory of all that I'd not accomplished or all that I had ruined, but now I knew that even though I had come here alone, it was not actually a problem, and at that moment I did not have to worry about anything at all.

Letters to the Doctor: The Old-Fashioned Doctor

Dear Doctor,

I am just feeling curious about something. Say what?! You're probably like, *Just curious? Not a crisis?! Nurse! Get in here and tell me who the hell is this fucking letter from!?* But here's what I'm wondering: If you could choose to be a doctor at any time in history, would you choose to be the kind of doctor you are now, with all of the fancy machines, or would you choose to be a doctor in the 1950s who smokes cigarettes even during an exam and whose answer to everything is the new wonder drug called amphetamines? Or would you be an ancient Sumerian doctor who taps a stake all the way into a live patient's skull with a scary little hammer (to treat the headache), and then calls it a day? If you could choose, would you be the kind of doctor that you are now? Because in my opinion, the kind you are now is definitely the best kind yet. I am certainly thankful for the medical care of today, which is so advanced that if you show up at the hospital and they don't even know your name, they still have all the machines and the labs and the medicines, and chances are they can fix you even *without* knowing your name. So, kudos!

But as for me, Doctor, sometimes I think I would want to be a doctor from the Jane Austen–y past. I suppose it is because I feel foolishly romantic about the idea of a doctor who isn't a total stranger? Don't get me wrong, I know those physicians were horrible at getting you well. They were always sticking leeches on people and boiling water for no reason and dripping droppers of nettle water out of dusty glass bottles, plus they took like five hours to get to you because their car was a wagon with a horse who had been asleep, and they would arrive in an overcoat that stank of mildew and B.O., and underneath that they had a long nightgown and most likely no underwear on, all to peer at you with a candle, put a gelatinous bug on your vein to suck your blood out, and then look exhausted *themselves* because of outrageously puffy under-eye bags like the PBS news anchors from the 1980s, and then after all of that they would say something like, "All we can do is pray."

They did not even know about hydration, and if they ever *did* save anyone, it probably *was* a god who did it, and *not* the doctor. And by "a god" what I mean is that in that moment,

Fortune stepped into the stream of Science, and somebody did not die.

Even though those doctors were fairly useless, one thing I like about them is that they knew your whole family and what had happened to all of them. I also like that a family member or neighbor would have to go "fetch" them. What a lovely community effort! I love stuff like that. I like that a brother or a father or a brave young niece would have had to ride a horse to go and get the doctor from the doctor's house. In a non-surveillance-y way, everyone knew where everyone else was, which I think is nice, plus it is nice that the animals had to help. It is nice to pair with an animal who would sense your need, rather than being alone, like with zero animals, and getting in your car in the middle of the night and having the song come on that you were blaring at yourself earlier that afternoon, and then seeing the plastic cup of iced coffee that you left in the car by mistake, now with melted ice and dead milk…All *that* certainly would not feel as cool as shouting, "Father! I'm off to Dr. Merriweather's!" and then bounding through the night air, finding your horse, throwing a leg over, slamming your junk on the back of the beast, yelling some rousing yell like "Yah!" and then riding so hard for quite a while in the dark of the night in the past.

Even in the past the road you would be on would be old, even for those times, and the woods too would feel old and that they were watching you, accompanying you on your worry, blessing the speed of your steed, and blessing your breathing, which after a while would match the pace of the horse. This breathing-in-sync would combine you with the strong innocent horse and give you a feeling of clean legitimacy: You are doing all you can to help, you are on the same team with this huge powerful animal, you know where to go, you are a person who is working with connection.

And eventually you would connect to me: I am the old-fashioned doctor in a long muslin shirt-gown, and after a relative fetches me I ride a wagon right to the patient's house, hustling gracelessly under the big round moon, bumping down the night road on wooden wheels through the dark where the trees and owls and freezing brooks are the boss, even more than the hemophiliac king that probably owns the land.

When I arrive at the bedside, I, the old and old-fashioned doctor, am winded from hurry and steep narrow house-stairs, and I am accompanied by all of the family members (no underwear on anyone), and a bunch of lanterns, and I definitely look upon my patient and have no fucking clue how to stop their diarrhea or asthma, and I scan their face with my candlelight and touch the knobs of their ankles for no reason but to see if maybe they are a random door to an answer, and I like that even though I have no way to solve the problem, I am still trying my best, and everyone is really glad that I'm here. I like that I would know this family well, that I could identify any of them from afar (even with my terrible eyesight that there are no real glasses for), like how you can tell if it is a swallow or a starling by the way they ride the air.

I would probably love saying, honestly, that the prescription is to *wait until dawn*. I am hoping that the fever will break like a big bag of water over the patient's fugued-out brain-holder of a head. I am hoping the patient's body will hold on to its sickness like a big hot salty tide, and just gush it out when the sun rises and pulls on that inner sickness-sea with some sort of magic/medicinal solar-gravity. It would all flood out and the patient would be clean of sickness, but drenched in sweat, and the healthy people would be so scared to change the linens, and I assume the mattress (made of hay and feathers?) would have to be burned up. And the family would rejoice and pledge to send me a goose at Christmas, and I, the old doctor, would ride back to my house in my nightgown and coat.

Arriving home, I drink a tipple of strong alcohol from a miniature glass cup. I retire to my rooms. I struggle while I release the rusty worm and broth of butt-stuff into a chamber pot. After all, I am me, but old and in the past, and I would most likely hardly be well inside of my own body. Then I sleep until my maid wakes me up to eat a gamey tiny bird, and I eat it, and I drink water from a metal pitcher, and I make pee-pee, and I go for a walk outside, and I write down what has happened to my patient and their family and therefore what has happened to me because we are all connected. We are so connected that even in the past, in a strict world of hats and manners, we have all seen each other in our nightgowns, knowing that our junk is just smacking around freely underneath, but we overlook that and tolerate it and stay together for the sake of the patient and our community. I am the old doctor, and I am never not connected to everyone around me, and they could, any of them, come to me at any time. Yet sometimes nobody calls for me and I am alone, and I live days between being called to wrap a foot up, or bring a baby from the womb to the basin and then to the breast.

Doctor, that's just me, though. Plus I know that I would not even be allowed to exist in this setting I have conjured, not without being burned as a witch or shunned as a slut, or just because I am Jewish. Maybe for being a fidget? Who the fuck knows, Doctor! People were spooked by everything back then.

Either way, it is something fun to think about. And I mean it from the bottom of my heart when I say that I'd love to know what you would choose.

Your friend and colleague (in a way/in my imagination),
Jenny

Single and Waiting for a Reply

My friends say that maybe he did not write back because he is very busy. Then I think, "I am never too busy for love, and starting lives." And then because I do not want it to be a rejection, I think maybe he is busy and that perhaps I do not really know what it is like to be busy. And then I think that perhaps I am not very successful? Maybe I do not know what it is to be really actually busy? But I think I do know, which of course is dispiriting, because it means that he is not more busy than I, which means you-know-what.

Storm

In Los Angeles, there is a house on a triangle-shaped plot that sticks into the road where two streets meet. On this V-shaped plot is an old Spanish-style house, and a proud husky who roams the big triangle. It is normal to be wary of a large dog who is basically a wolf. But when I used to smoke pot, I forgot that it was normal to be wary, and one day as I was walking by the triangle, I saw the animal, and I stuck my hand through the fence so that I could feel its face. The dog was peaceful and licked my palm with its pink tongue, and I felt for its necklace so that I could see what it was called. The dog was named Storm, which is wonderfully serious, and it made my day to know this.

Day after day I would visit this dog Storm. I would say "Hi,

Storm." And sometimes she would come right over and sometimes it would take longer if she was already doing something,
or sometimes someone else would be there visiting her through
the fence. One afternoon I was wasting time on the computer,
looking at old sweatshirts for sale. I do not tolerate junk, but I
do love treasures. I saw that there was a used but pristine white
sweatshirt, and in a dark dusky blue, right in the center of the
chest, it had been embroidered with the word "Storm." I purchased it right away, and I waited for a few days until it came. I
do not have any merchandise from concerts or movies, except
one huge T-shirt from a Paul Simon concert that my parents took
me to when I was eight years old. It was my first concert ever and
I was so overstimulated and unregulated that the moment I saw
all the lights and heard the horns, I threw up right away and had
to spend the whole concert in the first-aid tent with my mother
and her well-hidden disappointment. From the tent we heard
the muffled performance of "Bridge over Troubled Water," and
my mother said wistfully, "I love this song." The only other merchandise I have is this sweatshirt for Storm, and when it arrived
I put it on right away and walked over to her house.

If her owner had been watching, he would have seen a
non-barfing, grown woman come up to his fence and call to his
dog. Then he may have heard this woman say, "I'm your biggest fan, Storm, see?" And he would see that this woman was
wearing an embroidered sweatshirt with the name of his dog.
I was pointing at the word and trying to get Storm to notice,
but she didn't seem to care, and it almost hurt my feelings, but

then I remembered that dogs cannot read—like they cannot even recognize symbols—and I felt relieved that she was not displeased by my adoration but that she simply could not read. Because of Storm, I was able to say and believe "It's not personal" during a time in my life when all connections and rejections felt so *intensely* personal, and I felt glad to know myself as neither "rejected" nor "accepted," just the type of person who would make time in her day to visit a dog.

Letters to the Doctor: Prescription

Hi, Dr.,

I am just following up with a question about my eyesight and also my mind. I am looking at your last prescription and it says

For many things you can actually just remember that it's none of your business

5x a week: Don't be a grump

Daily: It is better when you don't take yourself too seriously

Is this what it says or should I see an eye doctor? These doses seem a bit high and taken a bit too often for me/my mind. I don't want to tell you how to do your job but I am wondering if you might want to review?

Have a great weekend!
- akjegf;kdgvkwjdfbvagljasehbks.;jfdgh;

The Pamphlet

My friend's friend told me about a book that brings you your soulmate. She said that she used this book and that she was sure that this was how she met Mike, who is her soulmate. She was speaking about it like, "Of course I am not a person who would just like *do a book* or something, like, *to get to my soulmate*, but I did do this thing, maybe half out of funniness and half out of light hopefulness, and whether you like it or not, or whether you want to believe it, I am now with Mike, my soulmate, who I met, I believe, because of this book."

It did not seem that outrageous to me, and she did not seem foolish. I knew her as a smart, stylish person and a great long-term friend to my friend, so I felt that I could trust her endorsement. Plus, the book was just a book, not a trick-book that encourages you to "buy coaching sessions" or "join our unique community," which is basically a cult. It was a book that cost about fourteen dollars, plus the shipping, and anyway I am not one to be tricked into being in a cult, because I am way too aware of how easy it might *be* to be tricked into a cult, and *because* I think I would be very vulnerable to being tricked into a cult, I make sure to know what to look out for.

When I got the book it was really just a pamphlet, and I sat up in my bed thinking, *But this is actually a pamphlet,* and it had things to fill in, like "What does your dream man do?" or "What does he look like?" Obviously, there was a moment of concern during which I said to myself, *Oh, hell no, you are not sitting here with a vibrator and a pamphlet.*

But then there was curiosity, because in all these years of writing things down and releasing a steady stream of wishing, I had actually never written down what the person of my dreams would be like.

I was interested to see what my answers were, and I thought that it was dear of me and not pathetic at all, in truth. I said to myself, *Are you lying to yourself?* I trusted myself not to lie if I was saying that I did not want to lie to myself. I thought that if any part of me was embarrassed about filling out a pamphlet in my bed, that I should not do it, and that if by any chance the pamphlet was charged with a kind of magic, that this magic would certainly *not* give me its power if I was acting embarrassed by it.

I did a check-over of myself, and I had only a small moment of embarrassment, and it passed so quickly that I had no remaining concerns.

I tried to fill out the pamphlet but I just kept writing descriptions of you, the stranger I met in Norway, the person unlike any other person ever, the person who I could not have. I would write in the descriptions, but then I would say, *No! You are making it be him! You have to open up, not just be stuck on the last person you saw!* But in truth I was simply putting down the qualities that I like, and they happened to be like you.

But later when I'd gotten exhausted by filling out the pamphlet and trying to make it be a general man and *not* you, I thought, *Okay, now I'm trying to make it **not** be him, but why can't it be him?*

I tried hard to make it not-you. The pamphlet was a little more than half filled out when I gave up and started my evening cleanup routine.

But my mind continued to distract me, stopping me mid dish-wipe or face-splash, directing me to one memory, as if fate itself was trying to get me to mark something: We had been in the front seat of a car in the Arctic Circle, parked in a supermarket parking lot. Our mutual friends were in the back seat. You moved a little bit, and the air delivered something my way, and I, my mammal-self, smelled the air, and my mouth filled with spit that my system made, and my mind sat up straight and asked: *What is that food/I want my food/What is that food/Why is there food here?*

The pamphlet must have opened up my mind like a bulkhead for that memory to run into, like how the tornado is coming and so the people run in, into the bulkhead and under the ground, into the deepest safest place, and they save their life.

The memory had been forgotten, but all of a sudden it was there, running at me, telling me, YES, THERE IS A PERSON! YES, HE HAS GREAT QUALITIES, BUT DO YOU KNOW THAT HE IS **ACTUALLY YOUR LIFE**?

The other half of the memory is that later that night in the Arctic, when you were cheeky enough to somehow get close, and you sat smushed up next to me on a fifty-year-old couch even though we were the only two people on the couch and you should have sat farther away, and your forearm pressed against my forearm, and I smelled my food again, and it was not simply "a food" but "my food," and it was as if I finally had the right answer to the question "What is your favorite food?" I realized with an electrifying breathlessness that what I smelled and wanted to eat up was actually the smell of your body. I knew it was *my food,* my favorite food.

Speared by this memory, and with my nighttime chores all half done, I had the unmistakable feeling that I had used an implement correctly, and the pamphlet did not need me anymore to do its work, and it filled out the rest of itself with writing that we are not able to detect. It was you, in the pamphlet, I could not stop it.

And although I am certainly thinking about it now, actually, after that night, I did not concern myself with the pamphlet anymore. I totally lost the pamphlet. The pamphlet was
by my bedside for so many months, but somehow it did not
find its way into a box when I moved all of my belongings into
your house.

Phase 2: True Love

Letters to the Doctor: Love

Hi, Dr.!

I am pleased to report that I have started to fall in love. Love is entering again. I am strings going from top to tail of the instrument, very tightly wound up. I am deep undersea beeps to navigate darkness and density. I am some chimes, too. I am a flock of clean breaths. My body lying down, my spine lying flat is the planks on the xylophone, many colors of planks.

Is this Health?

How long might I be expected to enjoy this?

I am revived, but will I be dead sleepy if this ends?

Just write back anything.

You know who this is from,

True Love: Garlic Chicken

I am in a restaurant and what I am eating is mostly the wine.

The woman next to me is telling her tablemate about Norway and Stockholm, and why it is worth traveling to these places. I want to tell them what I know about Norway (that in Oslo there is a theater just for puppets and that it was so fancy-looking that I said that it must be the opera house), and I want to tell them what happened to me there (that I made two friends laugh with my impression of a puppet-only-theater stage manager saying *FIVE MINUTES, MR. PUPPET*). I want to tell them that I met my new boyfriend way over there, and I am basically tilting over in my chair to interrupt them and excitedly say any one of these facts when a waiter comes and says *EXCUSE ME, GARLIC CHICKEN?*

And the woman says *ME.*

I lose my nerve, and furthermore how could I ever tell anyone what happened to me?

Would I say, "Excuse me, Garlic Chicken? I just want you to know that I believe that in the very north of Norway there is actually an invisible opening in the sky, not like an ozone-hole, but really a hole in the actual sky itself, and the hole opens to a sort of honey-lined atmosphere-womb in which dwells an energy that dripped down onto my skull and anointed me. Garlic Chicken, I want you to know that it dripped over my eyes, and closed them, and washed them, and then it dripped into my mouth, and helped me say the right things. When my eyes opened, they were washed, and I could see where my life needed to flow, and how I was going to need to change as a person if I wanted to get to where my life wanted to flow."

Would Garlic Chicken have clarity on all that or would there be questions? When I glance downward on the diagonal, I see that the woman named Garlic Chicken is reading a Kindle at the table where her friend is sitting across from her. But also, she is directing the conversation. I definitely want to ask what she is reading, but now she is talking about fashion-forward clogs and someone named Andrea, and I feel anxiety jump up as a frog-of-feelings in my chest. Now I am not eavesdropping as well as I was before, because I am wondering why this is always my deal, specifically: Why would I feel terrible just right now? What is touching me? What has changed?

When I start to listen again, Garlic Chicken is saying, "I'd do it if you wanted me to," which is such a kind thing to say to her friend, but she is reading a Kindle during everything happening here. She is reading her flat machine even while making this oath, so it is hard for me to tell how/if she actually cares about her tablemate. If she were holding a book, I would feel that she cares deeply and is simply comfortable with her friend, like maybe she might read aloud to her, flipping page after page, stopping for sips of this or that. But because what this woman holds is a flat little computer, I just feel like, "What the fuck, Garlic Chicken? Why did you leave your house with that? Why did you say *Okay, time to go to the restaurant* and then gather your keys, coat, wallet, and then add *this*?"

And what is on her tablet computer? Okay, it is Knausgård.

She tells her friend, "It took the world by storm."

I am spying on them and their situation is reaching out to me, but I am here alone and I am once again not sure if I know how to be with people, which is my guess at why the anxiety suddenly appeared. She is saying, "It's hard to figure out why good writing is good." She says she is deciding if she should or should not write. She says she did get props in college for her writing. I did not get any props in college. What *are* props, I wonder, and what happened to her when she got them in college? I am here alone, and I am watching other people interact, and I am noticing my own instincts, and it *is* making me doubtful about whether or not I am a normal person. But at least I *do* know that it would be wrong to interrupt them at this point and say, "Garlic Chicken, would you say more about what you experienced when you got props in college and what it was actually like, such as what people said or did? Like, how do you identify a *props?*" And I cannot interrupt them and ask, "Are *you* normal or am *I* normal?"

Then, instantly, twenty minutes have flushed out and I have eaten away at one of my actual hand-fingers and it is suddenly urgent that I use the bathroom and leave. I have unconsciously put my hood over my head. I leave the restaurant and run into my friend's boyfriend who is walking her dog, and I say the dog looks fatter, and am I immediately concerned with why I would say such a rude thing, and then he says, "Aren't we all?" and I say, "No, I am not," and then I get freaked out that I took him seriously, like he was weighing me, or asking for my weight or estimating it.

I walk up the hill to another friend's new house, and she shows me that she has finished decorating. One of the decorations is a giant painting that has glitter on it and is wonderful, and is by the first man who I wanted to have sex with, ever. I look at the glittery flower painting and remember lying naked on a bed in college, and how he ran his hands over my body the way you might touch a sculpture. But we are usually not allowed to make contact with the marble of a sculpture, and we never had sex, and years later I was on vacation with him and his boyfriend and we were all on drugs, and I was hugging a giant balloon in the shape of a champagne bottle, and they were naked in the pool, and I was in the pool with all of my clothes on and the balloon as my companion, and I thought, *Everything does work out right.* It was also on this same night that I made a fruit plate with the now ex-husband of the friend whose fat dog was being walked by her current boyfriend, in the present. Because we were on MDMA, the fruit plate took hours to make, and in the end, it consisted of one strawberry cut in half and a few raspberries splayed out in a design, and we presented it to everyone but of course it would have been traumatic to eat it. Having this memory come up only further confuses me about whether I am normal or understand how to be around other people.

My friend gives me a long hug and two pills to stop anxiety attacks because I had called her crying from the car the day before. She had said, "Are you crying? Are you in your car?" I tell her that I was racked with fear in the car yesterday, but nothing was wrong. I tell her that I am afraid that my new boyfriend will stop liking me because I had told him that I was drinking tequila on Saturday afternoon and then had a bath with my friend Mae, and some men wouldn't like that, and I've known some of those men, and generally I need to let go of worrying about what men like and don't like, but I really like this man and want him to like me, but then again, I'm not willing to hold myself back from what *I* like in order to make *him* like *me,* but clearly I'm still stressing about it. My friend with the sparkle painting on her wall tells me that I should not drive when I take the pills, and that things will seem clearer soon.

In the night that goes with this day, I have to do a show. I am not in what you might call "fighting form." In the bar, before the show, I start to get really sad and frightened that I actually cannot do this. It is not stage fright, it is fear of wanting the life that I am starting to possibly get. I want what I have, and I think, *What if I actually cannot do this? What if I get what I want and it just overloads me and I malfunction because I am not normal?* I do not want to do the show because I feel very serious about myself in a self-pitying and indulgent way, and my pants feel tight and I cannot remember pooping.

But I do the show, as one must when it is one's job to put on shows. We all have to do our jobs if we want to be able to buy our stupid fucking shirts and an infinity of alcohol. I go back to my house and I cry right as I enter the living room, which is not a new experience for the dog. I am able to rest and soothe myself a bit by saying things like, "It is only natural that you would feel very frightened by a chance at real happiness. But at least if it gets ruined, you can finally admit that you are bad at romance, and stop trying to partner up, and just become a mammal in clothes who does creative projects and travels the world. For example, you could go to the Seychelles."

The next morning, I talk on the phone with my new boyfriend. It is almost night there, where he is. He lives in another country, but not Norway. Carefully and with much fragility I tell him about my fear that I had turned him off by telling him about the cocktail and the bath with my friend, but all he says is that it "sounded like paradise," and then he says a number of other lovely and relieving things, and I have to stop myself from imagining us getting married, and telling him how much better he is than everyone else, because that is not the thing to do (because of how it creates pressure, and how that causes a very uncomfortable effect).

I have become so deeply attracted to the scent of his body that I have stopped shaving my armpits or wearing deodorant in the hope of smelling like him so that I can smell the smell that his body wears. I think it is a good sign that I am making myself into something more mammal in honor of him.

When I go to the airport to go on the trip with my new boyfriend (who is already at the first stop), I think about when we were on the phone, and that after talking about the tequila and the bath, he asked me, "Oh, do you want a checked bag, babe?" And when I recall this, the combination of him caring about my suitcase and that he, a healthy, vital, kind male is calling me *babe* creates a feeling between my legs that is so full that I squeeze my thighs together and chug water and pant like a little dog.

A man on the plane says *anything for the olives,* that is what he wants, and then he laughs at how much he loves olives and pings the joke again, saying, "Whatever the dish was with the olives!" He is just crazy for olives and he seems to like to show this about himself.

On this plane with the man who loves olives so much, I order a cocktail (which I love so much), and I think about Garlic Chicken and her computer tablet at the table the other day and, really, I find that I'm okay with it. We all have our reasons for going with our own flow, and I am glad that I never added myself to their conversation, because now I can see that it is none of my business, which is a normal thing to think! I had a cocktail in the bath with a true friend, and now I am having one in the sky itself while feeling happy for a stranger, and this is a sign that I actually *do* know how to be here, by myself or with others, because it is just really fun and good to do these things, and they are allowed, and people understand why I am doing them, and it is not disturbing. It is normal. And as a normal person, all I care about is smelling like a man who is so beautiful and rare that I can never tell him what I am doing (in terms of stopping my armpit shaving or stopping my deodorant so that I can smell like him), because I am being reasonable and thinking of the long game, and in the long game I tell him when we are old.

Letters to the Doctor: Dinner Party Seating

Dear Doctor, what the hell?

I have moved to a new place, and I brought with me all of my things, like my sweaters and my books and notebooks, my tangled jewelry and my bathing suit. My own house is still all the way over there on the other edge of the country, but I am slowly moving over here, perhaps forever, even as my just-planted trees start their lives at my own empty house. Over here, I have noticed more than a few times that there is a strange thing going on at dinner.

When we go to a dinner party at someone else's house, they tell us where to sit, and I do not mind assigned seating, or even stricter things like wearing a uniform at camp, but what is terrible about the assigned seating is that they split us up. They split the couples up and they do it on purpose, which means that they *force us,* which is a deranged thing to do to people at a party, to force them. That in itself is wrong, Doctor! Hold on for one moment, because I think I have to put the computer down because I can feel that feeling that you have before a piece of the skull caves in and the thoughts shoot out of the brain in a lasso of fire, drawing in whatever offends, drawing in the concept and holding it close so that I can char it and just char it all the way to powder.

Calmly, let me just ask: Why would you split a couple up against their wills? It is already so incredibly hard to come together and *become* a couple. One thing I would like to say before I die is that if people are going to make me sit somewhere that I was never planning on sitting, if they would like to pry me from my partner and make me suffer by my own shyness and shameful fear of instantly being forgotten by him if I am not right next to him, then I would like to reserve the right to fill my plate with food and then to fling it, full extension, out the nearest window. I will sit where I am assigned, and I will take deep breaths to the sound of shattering window glass. I will watch the grains of rice fall down like drops of rain, and just like the strange hosts who ignored that I came here with somebody, I will ignore that I chucked my china, and I will say nothing but comments about the weather, which happens to be raining rice.

This is where I am at, Doctor, and so I am wondering if you have ever prescribed anything like a Medical Companion Chair? Similar to when people get their Labradoodle a vest and paperwork so that the doodle can give the person love and support and sit by the person's feet on the carpeted floor of the airplane, and not down in the hold with the other howlers? Is there something like that, like a chair that I could have that *medically* is required to be next to my partner's chair? It seems like there could be that chair. Or you could invent one for me. I know that you could. I know that doctors can invent furniture. There is a special crib for babies now, invented by a doctor, and it holds them and rocks them and even makes a shushing sound so that the parent can rest too. The chair would also be good for my partner because he would benefit a lot from me being soothed. He could rest then, too.

I know that you will tell me that this is possibly something I could just get over on my own, by letting time pass so that I do not feel so vulnerable, and that I will gradually become a part of the community. Exposure therapy, I guess is what it is.

But if you could prescribe the chair, or create it and then prescribe it, that would be a relief. I am so prone to being affected by placebo, you could even lie and say that you are creating it or that the prescription is in the mail and I bet I would actually start to recover on my own.

Please do something, because I am on the verge of being "Remember that woman he brought, who broke the window?

She stood outside for a while, picking up shards of china and grains of rice, and ringing the doorbell for each shard or grain that she returned, and apologizing for every little piece."

Please help me, I am so intense,
"Girlfriend" Slate

On and Off the Island

I feel so bad for you! You must miss me so much because you left this morning to go to the island without me! Oh my goodness, you must be so wasted and drained about it! I assume you are trying to muster a pulse, even!

Before, I went with you to the island. I was by your side. If I did wander from you, it was only so that you could say, "Look at my sweet partner who goes around the island! Here she is on the dock, now she is on the boat. We hug and kiss, and here she is with her suitcase filled with smart clothes, and here she is up the stairs and back down because she forgot one boot! Cute! Here she is. There she is! The island is a circle in the sea, and she is somewhere on it, thank goodness!"

But now, no. You are on the small ferry with friendly strangers, and the waves are little chops, maybe not even any bigger than the fish themselves, and you are going over to the island, where you used to go by yourself, with strangers, but then I came along and proudly joined you, your co-host who had no responsibilities but to be your companion and help put out the breakfast.

You must miss me so much because you have left me here on the mainland and I was totally nice to you this morning and I am not, even as I sit here without you, cross or cold. I am a little nervous without you here.

I know that you must feel so good out there on the ocean, leading strangers to the island, and so you should miss me because I am happy for you. You should miss me, because I am not challenged by the fact that you are happy even though I am not there to be the center of that happiness. Before, I used to fear, "Maybe he is happy because I am *not* there, and he can have a break from me (a person who is stressful but also not important or necessary for his happiness)." You should miss me, because I got over that. But even when I write about how frightened I used to be, I still feel very sensitive about it. I still feel ashamed. And in a way, that is so sad! It is sad that we are able to be so frightened or hurt by other people from before, and then we arrive to whatever is "now" and we flinch because we are still conditioned to anticipate being hurt. And then, that is when we act out. And after that is usually when we become ashamed. It is difficult work to break that cycle.

One time, when we first got together, I had to go to New York City in the middle of our trip to the island. I do not remember how I got off the island, but I remember that I took the train to New York City and that I was very nervous to be apart from you. It used to seem to me that if I was not directly putting my face in front of your face, or making you feel good in some way, or giving to you, that you might lose focus and totally betray me. This was not because of any terrible qualities within you or anything you had done to me! It was because of things that had happened before I met you.

In New York City, I was sure that my absence, which was more than just leaving the room, which was a boat ride and a train ride and an elevator in a hotel away from you, would make something tragic happen. I was in New York City being interviewed about my performance as a cartoon dog, and I was saying over and over again how important it is to see a female character who is *confident and not sorry about that at all,* and *confident but still lovestruck,* and when the interview was over it was like my whole body started gagging, and my intrusive thoughts would trapeze and fail in their flights, and it was an acrobatic blood-bath in my mind.

"Something bad will happen."

"Something bad will happen and you are not lovable."

"Something bad will happen to prove that you are not lovable, but because you are not lovable you will not be told the truth about the betrayal. The only use that people can comprehend for you is that you are some sort of anchor, some sort of dead weight made out of a material that gives people cancer, I bet. And you will be lied to in all of the ways that lies can occur: by omission, to your face, because it is just easier to leave things out, 'for your own good,' or on purpose because you deserve it by being such a weak drip. And you will see evidence of how much you truly suck, because when you start sniffing around for lies, you will make people angry, and they will say that *nothing is wrong* and *you are making a fine situation into a bad one,* and this is *such a waste,* and *you are a disappointment,* and *why would a person do something like this?*"

And the answer that they will want is that you did it because you are crazy?

But you know that you are not crazy. You are just absolutely crazed, because you are so terribly afraid, and it is turning your mind into a stage on which the curtain is going up and down so fast like a mouth opening and closing, and someone to the side of this stage is playing a loopy and sadistic tune on the ivories, and the person on the stage is you, but with a huge head. And she has no lines but is just screaming as the curtain rips up and falls down and rips up and falls down.

So as I said, I was in New York City. I was wearing a green dress that was borrowed and had to be given back, plus the dress was too fancy for the occasion and so I felt foolish and it reminded me of my inability to achieve *casual elegance* and when I remembered this, I felt like a turd. "Wanting love does not mean that you lack confidence — in fact, it is that part of us that wants the love that is also the part that compels us to do our most courageous and unexpected acts," I was saying in English to a Spanish-language show about Hollywood News, in reference to my performance as the cartoon dog.

I was sweating a lot. It seemed to me that the island did not even exist anymore.

On the train ride home, I took a half of an anxiety pill that a friend had given me many months before, in case I needed it. I had saved it, but not responsibly. It was loose in the corner of my purse. I drank a beer on the train.

When I got back, I was woozy, and I had done such a number on myself in my interviews, talking about confidence but not feeling confident, that—in order to stop my constant internal fearmongering—someone would step up to comfort me, soothe me, tell me that I am lovable and worthy of being made to feel safe. And then, even if I received the care, I would have to bend over backward, as they say, to believe that *needing* this kind of care was not a sign that I was unlovable.

I felt that it was all just such a mess, just such a terrible mess. All I had really eaten that day was the half of the pill and the bottle of beer. Carrying my suitcase across the flagstone in front of the house made me fall down. I skinned my knee for the first time since I was a child. There was a lot of blood all over my knee and down my leg.

I went inside with blood on my leg and went right to the bathroom because you were coming to meet me in just a minute and I did not want you to see my wound at its worst.

I was shy to see you when you came off the boat and into

the house. I saw you see me. You said something so nice that when I try to remember it I can only feel the feeling of when you see something peaceful and gorgeous, like a pitcher of water filled with flowers on a table set outdoors for lunch (maybe in France?), and you cannot believe that you have traveled so far, to such a lovely place that is real. You kissed me right away. You smelled the place under my ear, at the juncture of my jaw.

Nothing bad had happened on the island while I was away. So much bad had happened to me in my mind while I was in New York City, but it only came from inside, and it was only in the past. That was not the best news, but it was sort of good because it was like, "Okay, we can move her because we know where the injury is." You are not supposed to move a hurt person when you do not know where the injury is. You can kill them by moving them, or paralyze them by moving them. You have to understand that they are down but they are not out. I was down in New York City. I was out of my mind inside of my mind, but I was not a lost cause.

You walked me down the dock and took me to the boat. I sat behind you like we were on a motorcycle. My knee was really hurting a lot but I still let myself bend my legs. *She can be moved, she won't die if we move her.* I pressed my whole upper body against your back.

You should miss me because years later I have a tiny scar from that rather large wound, and it is nothing but a soft, light marker of time. You should miss me because you are all alone on the island, and I love you so much, actively I love you, and

I am here writing this down, only with love, and with no fear of betrayal, just regular-sized fears like *I will twist an ankle and ruin my autumn,* or *I'm forty and the only acting role I'll get is to play the voice of a broken antique cartoon lamp,* or *a mouse will continue to hide bits of our dog's food in an inaccessible part of our oven and start (another) fire.* You should miss me because I am aware that I am controlling about the tidiness of our house, and I am thinking about adjustments on that, but not many. I do have to be who I am.

You should miss me because I am proof that things can specifically grow and change when you give good care, and you are the care, and I am the care, and when you think of that, of how hard we have both tried in different ways to care for each other, you should miss me. Honey, you should miss me because I know you as the person who looked past my fits of fright and helped me through to now. You should miss me because even though I was rabid with fear simply because we had fallen in love and it was worth everything to me, I was still strong enough to see my way out of the repulsive rapture of low expectations.

On the boat back to the island, I was very conscious of how quickly my dread retreated. I recalled that my sister had said, "You can't just solve this problem by never being apart." It was true. She was correct. As our boat left the dock, I knew that my knee was not better yet. In fact, it took a really long time to heal. Then we were making a rounded and wide turn away from our house and our dock and we were speeding into the open ocean. You were looking straight ahead and you started to go fast. You said without any prompting, "You just make me really happy. You just make me really happy."

I will always be sorry for the ways I terrorized myself and it ran onto you, but I also know that for a while, I really could not do anything but what I was doing. I was limited by injury.

You should miss me, because I miss you the second you go through a door, or into a car that I am not in, or across the water, or to sleep. You should miss me, because I remember every kind thing you have done, because I keep a record of how generous you are and I know this record is a compilation of truths. Miss me because of the heights that I scaled to get to you, from the bottom of my confidence, slowly and scarily up, up, up to the top, where reality is.

Phase 3: Pregnancy

We Have to Stop: Fantasy Psychology Session

ME: So there was a bone that I wanted —

PSYCH: Actually, is there a different way that you could begin?

ME: Yes. Sure. There was a fish bone that I wanted that was a present from Ben when I first moved here.

PSYCH: Uch, this is just really hard for me, Jenny. Okay, whatever, let's try: Did he give you, like, a single bone in an empty box?

ME: Ha! Oh, no, no, no, sir! Sorry, just to be clear, I'm not calling you sir, although, do you like when people call you sir? If you have kids, like, do they call you *sir* or *Dad*?

PSYCH: Let's keep this on you. Let's talk about the...I guess the bone, I guess...

ME: Oh yeah, okay, so we were on the beach and my fiancé *saw* the bone and gave it to me because it was clean and smooth and dry and had a lovely shape.

PSYCH: Okay, just checking.

ME: I keep it on the shelf above our bed, and recently it fell behind the headboard of the bed, before we left for our trip that I didn't want to take.

PSYCH: Why didn't you want to take the trip?

ME: Because I was afraid that we would sleep in a bed that had a bad smell because it was in a cabin by the sea, and as you know I suffer from a repulsion about mildew.

PSYCH: Yeah.

ME: So I tried to get it from under the bed.

PSYCH: Why couldn't you just leave it under the bed?

ME: Because I don't like it when you get back from a trip and the house is frozen in the different types of laziness and disregard that were going on when you left. When you return from a trip, you have a pretty good chance at being, like, "new" in a way? And so I thought that everything should be perfect for when we got back. It's a way of feeling renewed and energized. If the bone had been lying in the thick, soft under-bed dust, we would be connected to that period of letting things slide. If we got back and it was clean and in its place of honor on the shelf above the bed, our entire life would be easier because of that light feeling of everything being in order.

But I forgot that I'm too big now because of how pregnant I am, and the bone was out of reach, and so I used an electrical cord to snag it and drag it out, but I still had to shove myself under the bed a bit, and because I was so close to having the bone in hand, I forgot about what I am presently like, physically, and I impulsively squished myself toward the bone, and felt a horrible feeling, a dangerous feeling of squishing my baby, or so it felt, and then I felt something that no person (especially a pregnant person who will soon have to be a parent and in my case a "mother") wants to feel, which is the distinct shame of being a fucking foolish idiot.

PSYCH: Uh-huh, okay. You know what I would say about that type of self-characterization.

ME: Yeah.

PSYCH: Okay.

ME: On the drive to the trip that I didn't want to take, he mentioned that he wanted a mirror from the general store, and it was a carved wooden mirror and he thought it would be perfect for the baby's room. The way that I feel about that is that the house is already filled with heavy dark objects, and that it all seems self-gnarled rather than hand-carved, and I don't want that in my baby's room, because the gnarls make me think of talons, which are basically nothing but prehistoric feet-teeth. Like, if you think about what talons are, that is what they are.

PSYCH: Interesting. I do agree that talons are akin to feet-teeth.

ME: It's dead-on. In terms of the mirror, he said he liked and wanted it, and he showed me the picture of the mirror. I said to whatever part of myself that was available within my own rigidity, "He's very sweet and he said he wants it," and I decided to look sort of *over* the image he showed me, and *toward* that aim of letting him be happy, like when you look over a river to the house on the other side.

PSYCH: My daughter has a house on a river.

ME: (*Instantly screaming*) OH MY GOODNESS, PLEASE NEVER TELL ME ANYTHING ABOUT YOURSELF EVER AGAIN THOUGH! (*Beat.*) So I was like, "Do this! *Be* this! *Let* him!" But then I did see the picture of the gnarled mirror, and how it looked so heavy, and I made an involuntary noise, which obviously made me feel terrible about myself.

PSYCH: In what way?

ME: That I am selfish, and peeved all the time, and ungenerous and inflexible, and that my sense of aesthetic pleasure clashes profoundly with his because he is a New England WASP and I am a South Shore Jew who has always thought that it's weird to fetishize old British and Christian culture, especially since a lot of it has discriminated against Jewish people, like saying that we are obsessed with money, when anyway, everyone is obsessed with money except for the Buddhists.

PSYCH: Peeved, ungenerous, inflexible. Are these qualities that you think a mother should not have?

ME: Me?

PSYCH: Yes, I am talking to you.

ME: Okay, just checking. Anyway, then we went by the store on our way to the trip and I acted like I was running in for a snack, but my main act was that I found the mirror, which looked like a prop from a play about teen sorcerers, and I told the lady to hold it for two days while we go on vacation, and I told her my name, and she told me that this object was what I think is a very high price for a piece of absolute crap, and I did *not* make a noise even though I had one coming. I kept it in, which was encouraging to me at the moment.

PSYCH: Okay, I hear that, but we have agreed to work on *not* holding in your noises, right?

ME: No, I know, but if I *had* made the noise, then she would have thought that I was a bitch.

PSYCH: Are you worried that your baby will think you're a "bitch"?

ME: I don't see how that's relevant.

PSYCH: Well, we haven't yet discussed what you said at the start, about how no parent wants to feel like they don't know what they're doing, or in your words, "like a fucking foolish idiot."

ME: (*Stupidly defensive*) Let me ask *you* something, okay? Why do non-pregnant people think that pregnant people only want to talk about being pregnant? It's especially offensive coming from a male. I just want to talk about the mirror and me holding in my bitch-noise.

PSYCH: Okay, and what else could you have done besides holding the "bitch-noise" inside?

ME: I could have said something.

PSYCH: Great, like what?

ME: You're making me really upset.

PSYCH: Okay, or you could have asked a question about the surprisingly high price of the mirror, right?

ME: No, no, *you right now* are making me upset.

PSYCH: We've been here before, Jenny. There is a pattern I notice in which you attempt to skip over your negative feelings. Let's talk about why you're feeling upset.

ME: (*As if not hearing him*) And so while we were driving to the trip…

PSYCH: Let's pause just for a moment—

ME: *And so while we were driving to the trip, please, this is what I am talking about right now,* I planned, in my mind, that I would go back to the store by myself when we returned, and that I would purchase the mirror and put it up in the bathroom that is for the baby who will arrive in the winter, and I thought that I would stick a note on it, to my fiancé, telling him something nice, and I would look in the mirror and like what I see: my easy-to-look-upon face framed by something outside my comfort zone, hung in place by my own good intentions. And also I actually *did* like the trip and I am actually *really nice* and everything is *fine*! Okay! We have to stop!

PSYCH: Jenny, I'll just remind you that it is fine to be in conflict and it's normal and healthy to be intimidated by what you're undertaking in becoming a parent—

ME: Oooop! We have to stop.

PSYCH: Jenny...

ME: I need to be the one to say it! Let me! *Let me.* This is the only place where I can lay down any type of boundary and mean it and not feel immediately in danger of being judged and inevitably abandoned—

PSYCH: A session ending at the agreed-upon time is not a judgment or an abandonment—

ME: YOU BETTER SHUT UP RIGHT NOW! I never get to be the one to draw the line because I am not confident enough, but I can at least practice it here, especially because all these narcs in the baby books say your baby needs you to *hold boundaries,* and if you can't fix my personality at least you can fucking let me practice that stupid fucking super-threatening boundary-thingy in here, so...just...fucking...*I'm the mom and I'm the one that says that We Have To Stop For Today!* (*Deep exhale.*)

PSYCH: We have to stop.

ME: (*After a beat*) You messed up by saying that your daughter has a house on the river. You aren't supposed to let me know anything.

PSYCH:—

ME: We have to stop.

Stork Dream: Scroll

The Stork appeared soundlessly, using a long shadow in my bedroom as the entry point. I remembered something long forgotten: *Oh right, the baby will be delivered by Stork.* It stepped from the shadow as if I had called to it by realizing the truth of how my baby would arrive. Its feathers and straw-like legs were strobing with filaments, threads of metallic light. The creature-deity took an hour to walk from the closet to the side of the bed. I watched it the whole time, and there were no sounds anywhere. When my Stork reached my bedside and its body was close to mine, I smelled rose geranium so strongly that I felt like someone was pouring into me a liquid that should only be sipped or tincture-dropped, but it was pouring faster than I could gulp it. I was lying down and I looked up at the face of my Stork. I saw that its beak was brushed gold, and that this golden beak was not a mask, but organic, and living on the Stork—like it was alive the way that coral is alive? The face of the huge bird was turned to the side and I saw the moonlight in the gold of the beak, the moonlight lying in strings in all of the little brushed crevices in the gold. I saw the light, but to see it was to also hear a small, soft, deep bell.

My Stork would not make eye contact with me yet because it was too early, not time for the baby to be delivered. I squinted at what I was trying to see and I thought, *Holy fuck, is this thing smoking?* I saw that what was in its beak was a steaming scroll, like a cinnamon stick, but illuminated in that thick way that an ember is lit, how a coal's light is deep in there, and slow. It opened its beak to let the scroll fall into my open hand, and when the beak opened I heard the sound of light itself, which was kind of like the sound when people "play the saw" but louder and only for me to hear, and only a half a second long. The instant that the scroll touched my skin, it became the same temperature as the rest of me, and my Stork blinked off and it was there no longer, and my consciousness nested warmly into a circle of sleep. When I woke up, I noticed that I had written on the notepad I keep on the table. I had written on the paper and rolled it up tight like I was about to shove it into a bottle. When I unfurled the paper, it said, "When you ask for a baby, you call out to danger, as the two are braided together. It is best to see the beauty of the braid. Danger does not mean disaster."

I was still holding my little scroll when I put my foot down onto the bedside rug, and I saw for a moment the lit-up imprint of a large bird foot. It wrapped around my own foot before zipping up the inside of my shin, my knee, my thigh, and right up into my vagina and into the amphitheater of my pelvis. I thought that this was the craziest thing yet about waiting for the baby: Now I was going to have to spend who knows how long with *this* thing in my pelvis, because I had no idea how to get it out. Honestly it is all so complicated and elaborate but also totally exact that it often seems ridiculous, preposterous even, and so I just laughed. And then I *actually* woke up, and the sound that took me from dreaming to awake was myself laughing at how bizarre this experience is of making a lifeform while being a lifeform. I woke myself up laughing, and the laughter was like a string of bells being pulled from inside of me.

The Drive-In

We drove one and a half hours to the drive-in and we saw the movie *Ghostbusters.*

Inside the car, at the drive-in, while we were watching *Ghostbusters,* it was hard to find a comfortable position because I was very pregnant and I was convinced that if I put my calves on the dashboard and pressed the soles of my feet onto the windshield, it would break off from the front of the car, that I would break the car with my body, and then we would have to get home some other way, and how, during a plague? This is how strong I believe my body is, but only in terms of how it could cause destruction. But how strong I believe my body is when it comes to things like being useful (like carrying a flat of twenty-four seltzer cans), that level of strength rings in at "actually not ever strong enough." Strong enough to cause an expensive catastrophe but not strong enough to carry bubbly drinks in slight bulk.

In the movie, the actor Bill Murray plays an irreverent scientist named Peter Venkman, and the first time we see him, he is using pseudoscience to try to fool his much younger female student into most likely doing "it" with him, or maybe they would just make out and he touches her boobs? Or maybe he would pressure her into giving him a blowjob? Or just full sex? And it is weird because we laugh at how he is behaving, but he does indeed have an aim, something he is working hard to get, and none of the outcomes feel very funny at all, and it would really ruin this movie if he actually got his way. This is a classic movie *that I still love.* Somehow the female student is also horny about the whole thing? But for no reason that I could detect? And coming from someone who has literally been able to become horny over things like marshes swelling with high tide, unpacking boxes in a new house, and also things like cruel, traditionally unattractive men, and also cruel, traditionally *attractive* men (and many other types of men, and occurrences in the natural world, like volcanoes and mosses), it is telling that I just could not crack the code on this one, like, *why* is she into him, except that a man *wrote* that *the female student is attracted to Professor Peter Venkman,* and so it was depicted? I guess power could be the answer, that he has power, and maybe she finds that attractive? He's funny — that is always pretty hot—but also, he seems like a zealous liar, which is scarier than any of the ghosts that will be busted in this film.

In this scene, Peter Venkman is interrupted while he is, I guess, trying to fool this student into sex? But he "loses her" the way that you might lose a fish off the line. And this is supposed to be funny, *was* funny to me all of the times I had seen this scene until right then. But now I thought, *If you saw a news story right now about a professor at Columbia who was doing fake ESP tests on students, and shocking the non-female students with electricity when they got answers wrong, all so that he could touch the boobs and privates on some students' bodies, you would think, "Oh my god, this is so bad. This is crazy. This is so fucking deranged."*

We were watching the movie and I started to become upset. It was very hard to see the joke as funny anymore, and it made me clutch the area on my body that is the landing pad for where the lifeform was gradually arriving. It made me put my hands there to mark it with something else, like sort of a primal protective palm print. I was putting my hands there but then I kept watching the movie, and I *did* and *do* like this movie, generally. I like the movie, that is not really what this is about. I was drinking orange soda in the dark of our car, and the windows were up because the mosquitos were gnarly, and then of course I would burp and have to open a window and I would feel bad for my fiancé, who might have smelled the burp or gotten a bite from a mosquito.

We watched quietly, and an unexpected, webbed tension formed in me during a scene where Peter Venkman enters Sigourney Weaver's (Dana's) apartment without her wanting him to. He just pushes his way past her and then he is totally in her house. *Then* he starts spraying mist from a sprayer all over the place, and she asks about the sprayer and he will not even tell her what the equipment is. Then he comes on to her, and she has to push him out of her apartment, and he asks for a kiss while wedging himself back through her almost-slamming door, and she has to push him out by putting her hand on his face and pushing his face.

I looked at the screen and saw the green ghost named Slimer slamming down discarded room service while also being dead and dripping with ectoplasmic gunk. I thought about how much I feel like Slimer sometimes: driven but technically dead, obsessed with room service and easily agitated, afraid of being thrown back into a darker realm, hoping to just live with the alive people who think that I am gross and that I make every situation about myself. This is what happens when a ghost is anywhere. It is all about them.

We drove one and a half hours to see the movie, and it was supposed to be a treat to take our minds off the plague, but I could not stop thinking about how I would feel if I were Sigourney Weaver's "Dana" and this whole thing was happening to me. Dana is just trying to play her cello and buy sensible groceries, and then this guy is so terrible and annoying to her and he won't go away! But she's charmed by him anyway, and if that were me I would blame myself for "letting him" push his way in.

Years later, when he would turn out to *essentially* be an asshole (rather than a charismatic scientist who busts ghosts), and not very smart after all, and certainly not kind, and a zealous liar who is pathetically bent on trying to get people to notice him for being a Ghostbuster (while I would have impulsively thrown away my professional cello career because it did not work with supporting *his* whole thing), that is when I would realize that there is not one reason to continue having a relationship with him. I would have that feeling of wanting to make up for lost time.

It would all end with me in my fall outerwear, standing among my suitcases, not accepting his wretched apologies, knowing that I am nothing to him at this point but a stand-in for his "bad mommy" and the fear he feels because he has been given a lot of power that he secretly suspects he does not deserve. I would weather the traditional storm of insults like "You are a stuck-up bitch" and "You think you're so kind and virtuous, but you are vicious" or the weird one, "I treat you like gold!" Or the scary one, "Everyone in your family is lying to you and you are spoiled," and the kicker: "I've changed my whole life for you!" I would know that it was useless to say anything because he would understand nothing, retain nothing. Yet I would still stand there by the door to the rest of the world and make my "listening face" while secretly thinking about how excited I am to go and meet the person who is about to show me the nice one-bedroom apartment that I could stay in for the next six months because that person is moving to Prague or Morocco. And even though I had already given far too much, I would give Peter Venkman one final mercy and say, "I wish you well." Because in the end, it is hard to hold boundaries against narcissistic misogynists if you are like me and have been deeply conditioned to be afraid of being called "mean," so sometimes you end up doing things like giving them time over the phone, but you do something else while they talk because they are so boring (for example, you organize a drawer or fold laundry), and then you remember that you actually can leave at any time, and that your schedule is private, and so you say you have to "jump off" and you do not say why, which kills them a little because they want to own everything including your schedule that they don't care about, and then because you are a bit nervous about putting down the boundary, *you wish them the best,* you say. You say that *you wish them well.*

But then I thought that if this was the turn I was going to take with this narrative, I should take it all the way. *Ghostbusters* is a true classic, and I couldn't let it end with a thud! And so I imagined that as "Dana" I would really floor it. There would be a flashback montage of all the scenes when Peter Venkman would not leave when asked, when he pushed past protestation or a flat-out no, when he was annoying, when he separated me from my friends and values, and there would even be a flash-back to the initial scene with the student, and then the montage would end, followed by a scene in which I bolt up in bed after replaying all of that in my mind, and then I would hail a taxi to the Ghostbusters' firehouse, where he'd had to move back in because I kicked him out of the apartment and then I moved to a *new* place that he had never been inside of at all, which was immediately refreshing and restorative for me, Dana.

I would go into the building and wake him up by tenderly stroking his face. He would wake, confused and then slightly horny when he saw *my* face. I would see that he immediately assumed that I was coming back to him. He would assume this because he was unable to ever learn or change, had brittle self-esteem, but still an astounding sense of entitlement. And I would relish his misunderstanding as I slowly lowered my face to his and I would say in a whisper, "I actually *don't* wish you well."

And he would say, "What?"

And I would smile and walk backward and look at him and say, "I said I *did*? But actually I *don't*. I don't wish you well."

And he would accuse me of having a breakdown and needing to sit and drink a glass of water, but I would not care, because I would know that I was obviously experiencing a break*through*, and the audience would know too. And he would listen to me from his stupid little bed as I said the rest, all while moving slowly toward the thing where they keep the ghosts stored. As I ambled through his place of professional achievement, I would say:

"I hate thinking about you. Thinking about you only begets other disgusting thinking."

The camera would float with me as my voice got louder because I was moving farther away and I needed him to hear me. He would be sitting up in bed at this point. I would yell out: "Peter? Can you hear me? A sulfuric wind blows through you constantly! You *do* have bad breath and you have it a lot, and I lied to you about it because you are too fragile to even handle the truth, which is that you have a human body and it *is* fallible!" And at that, he would spring out of bed and clumsily put on a bathrobe because, after all, this is a movie from the eighties and they always wear bathrobes. He would start speed-walking to try to find me in their facility. I would be sauntering toward the ghost-holder thing. I would be singsonging the truth about him: "You were never curious, not even one time. You were mean, and predictable, and you had bad style and you were one of the worst kissers I have ever kissed!" He would yell, *"WHAT?!"* And he would pick up the pace and trip on some boxes and run up the stairs after me. I would look down through the stairwell at him and yell:

"You! Are! Boring! And you are *vain*, so vain, I've never seen anything like it!" And I would run. And he would run! And then he would catch up to me and my hand would be on the lever and I would be about to release a shit-ton of angry ghosts right at him.

He would say, "Dana! Dana?! You don't understand what you're doing, honey! You don't need to do this." And I would scream, "I understand everything and that is why you hate me! Get away from me! Get the fuck out of my line of sight, get out of my mind, get out, get out, get out! How *dare you*! *Get the fuck away from me!*" And then there would be a moment where everything was held in midair. And then I would pull the handle down and smile at him and the *Ghostbusters* theme song would kick in right then, and the ghosts would gush out at him and he would scream "Noooooo!!!!!" while they pushed him back and away from me.

And then I figured that the credits would roll over a montage of Dana playing her cello at a prestigious outdoor concert in Central Park, having a glass of wine with her friends from the orchestra, and doing other things like taking in the delivery of a huge fruit basket with a card that makes Dana laugh so fucking hard because her life is nice and so are her friends, and we would see her squeezing the moisture out of the sponge in the kitchen after the dishes are done and then turning out the kitchen light. And we'd see her in her own bathrobe, sitting in the dark of her living room with more wine, looking out the big window and into the evening, and there would be ghosts floating everywhere in the air outside, because there are. Maybe Slimer is her pet now?

Getting away from Venkman might be a bit of a scrape, but Dana would hold the line, and then she would be free. Of course, this would make *Ghostbusters* into a very different film, but I feel that it all works rather well, actually.

We drove one and a half hours in the dark to get back home. I tried to listen to the music, and then to open the window to hear the bugs, and just take it down a few notches because I thought that it might not be right to share the radiation of my inner-cinema with the lifeform as it built in me. And then when we got home, the dog was despondent of course. She is like me, and so she really hates to be left alone.

If the dog is at all secretly spiteful (which I doubt), but if she is, she would be soothed just a bit to know that I got a lot more than I bargained for at the drive-in. And since she loves me, she would also be happy that I experienced a downpour of difficult feelings, but that then I took those feelings and I made my own secret, personal art by reimagining the plot of the movie, and after that, I self-soothed so that my internal environment could be peaceful for the lifeform that I was creating. My dog would be pleased that I set the fire and also put it out when I had had enough. She would feel happy for me that this whole experience has been recorded here as useful, rational, and engaging criticism regarding a classic piece of American cinema that still has many strong points but also some troublesome blind spots.

The Night Rope

While I sleep, my hand becomes very strong, extra-strength, and the fingers bend in and put pressure on my palm. I am dreaming that I am holding on to a rope. It is a hollow rope, a rope like a tube in my hand, and it is going outward, beyond the bed, and out the window and over the water and into the other dimension where the spirit of the little lifeform is waiting in the roaring realm of non-bodied, non-form, total-spirits. My rest-rhythm knows to hold on to the rope in this downtime, when I do not worry but when I let my brain be wild with impressions and nonsense. While I am dreaming, my body with the womb-in-use is the port that lights up for her incoming consciousness. My body now is not the bay of doubt it can sometimes be, but a harbor of well-being. As I draw closer to waking, the rope rubs itself against my palm until it turns from rope to ray-of-energy, and this ray runs into my veins, and stays reaching far into my body while also still reaching out to the other side, far away.

When I wake up, I know that the dream is over, and yet I am still tethered. I connect to the lifeform in my dreams, I am never not with her now. The most secure attachment is done, not just through what I must do in the life to come, but also in the work that I do in my dreams now while I am making her. I pull her a bit closer to this side every day, and I keep the light on at the landing spot. I make her body. I keep pulling through the dark, until she is filled with enough of a draw to make her spirit leap into her body, which is in my body, and then into our life that we will have together. When she gets here, she will take this rope back, and her life will be officially hers, and my hands will be empty so that I can hold her.

The Raccoon

We caught the raccoon in the night after the houseguest said he heard it trying to open the door.

I did not want to see it in the cage because I specifically did not want to see his soft body and arms, like he had put on a sweater before this happened. You put on a sweater to do something normal, like going to the post office, or walking from a smaller room into a larger room in your home in the winter. To put on your sweater, to do that kind act for yourself, expecting nothing but to move and observe and do an easy task, and then to be in fact lured into a metal trap with a slanted door? I did not want to deal with that image. I did not want to see a raccoon with the little hands and the naturally expectant mask and perfect face.

The raccoon had been tricked into the trap. After an evening of nightmares and the feeling that I was sleeping wrong—meaning that the blood was not going to the small and currently forming lifeform inside my abdomen—my fiancé told me that he had caught Justin, which is what I had named the raccoon on the first night that I saw him drinking the pineapple syrup from an upturned can that he had chosen for himself and then taken from the trash bin with his little hands. This little robber with his tongue and small gulps and swallows! I know that it must have tasted so good to him. When I named Justin, I used his name right away via the thought *Justin loves canned fruit in syrups, and so do I.*

My fiancé told me that he'd caught Justin, but he was going to sleep a bit more before confronting him. I put my mind to work right away, picturing the raccoon in the cage: He is watching the morning close in on him like the high tide. In the morning, a high tide of light creeps up into the shore of the day itself. I like very much to watch it from our bed, and so of course this makes me imagine watching the day begin through the grid of the cage. I am feeling what Justin is feeling. I am feeling the instincts in the animal, and that the instincts cannot complete themselves. How much frantic discomfort he feels calling in his core: *Run away very fast, be out, be out, be out, be free, do whatever I want! The sun becomes too pushy, and I feel in the clock in my body that it is time to rest and wind down, and sleep the sleep of the winded and free animal, and be in big spaces. I am made to be just my small size, but in the biggest of spaces. Me and then the night sky, that is the right pairing of my smallness with a largeness, and I am made to be totally unrestrained! What is happening to me in this cage?!*

I feel my bones ache when I touch the charged current of raccoon-feelings. Beset by the advancing daylight, the raccoon feels a creepy-deathly feeling: *I cannot do my deep-things, the instincts themselves ache when not completed. This is the end of me, maybe because I will die, sure yes I can feel the edges of my demise, but the horror is definitely because I am alive and I am prohibited from completing my deep-things.*

I went and made the coffee even though it was very early and I knew I would most likely have to make another pot when my fiancé woke up and when the houseguest woke too. The house-guest is a person who I love, but the houseguest leaves tea bags all over the surfaces in my house, and when I find them all I can think is, *Your mother taught you this. She taught you this by silently cleaning up your small hot wet bags that you use to make your warm drinks for yourself. She facilitated this. But now your mommy is not here and so I am picking up your small hot wet bags because I am being hospitable, but also sort of pressured into being quiet about this because otherwise I will ruin the vibe, and here we have a very clear case of what some men are allowed to do and be, because in the end it is just not worth the fucking time to explain to a giant male baby who thinks that they are an adult that they have to take literally four seconds to put their small hot wet bag in the greater bag of trash. That is where it goes! In the trash. This is what you are doing: leaving trash around my house. If it is not a big deal, if I am being uptight, if it is not a big deal and you are such a chill, strong person, then handle this one yourself and put your trash in the trash.*

It is very bad that the mother always gets blamed, especially because by cleaning up the small hot wet bags and not saying anything, I am doing just what the mother was doing. I am not teaching him how to behave otherwise, but of course, how the fuck is that my job, among the other jobs that he has created for me?

Also I will soon be a mother and that means that I will eventually be blamed.

Yet, the idea that I would go to a man's house, while he is all day all night growing *another* lifeform *inside* of his own body, and that I would leave small hot wet bags on his side tables, and in drained cups that get left on the coffee table as if the Great Mystery itself will somehow seize the small hot wet bags at any moment and waft them into infinity, well, that is totally preposterous. It is me, sir, I am the Great Mystery that makes your small hot wet bags invisible. And infinity is a perfect way to describe where the silence of my repeated labors deposits itself, somewhere between the trash can and the sink.

And you know who taught me how to clean up after *myself* and be tidy in other people's burrows? *My* mother. So it is one to one: one mother blamed, one mother thanked. And what do we have here? A raccoon in a cage, a woman in the house, a lifeform gaining ground inside the woman, two men, and a troublesome accumulation of small hot wet bags that, let's face it, represent a much larger issue that is one hundred percent real, and is compounded by the fact that if you bring it up, everyone feels allowed to dislike you.

I went back to the bedroom and I sat up in bed with my half a cup of coffee, because that is all I was allowed to have per the doctor's orders. I was not allowed to be jacked up on anything anymore, except the operatic intensity that I felt when I tried to imagine a real future in which I had no choice but to erupt a baby from my own vagina or be cut open in an emergency. That jacked me up for sure. I looked out the window and to the water and I thought, *Even if we didn't kill Justin—which obviously we won't but he doesn't know that—and let's say we drove the trap to the zoo and made some sort of a deal with the zoo and put him in the zoo as one of the residents there, he would still be trapped and he would be a dented and dimmer version of himself.* The pulse of the instincts—the true purpose of each creature—is fully alive underneath its oppression, and that is why it is sad to see the animals in the zoo. Not just for all of the reasons that you could list right now, but because you see the wildness shut inside of the animal itself. That they are made to contain the expanse of their own limitlessness, a limitlessness that is wildness itself, that they are made to domesticate their wildness inside of their bodies while they are forced to live in a fabrication of their world. This must hurt so badly and smell so wrong. When I even think about the sentence *You are not allowed to leave* I begin to choke a bit, and I smell something bad, like deep in the olfactory of my spirit itself I smell something like spoiled chicken salad in the trash can. I am not allowed to even eat *fresh* chicken salad, doctor's orders.

I told myself not to upset myself and to try to end the thought when the coffee was over, but then I started taking really small sips to cheat against myself. I was remembering one time when I was stoned in the zoo, and I rushed up to an enclosure, and I was excited because I did not know what it was, like, *What's in there?* I could not see anything, and then I realized that it was just ducks, or "simply for ducks" — a "duck thing" — and with obvious disappointment I said, "Oh, it's just ducks." I said it out loud, and I have always felt bad about that, that the ducks all heard it. They were stuck in a place that is totally a fake place, real water but a fake pond. I knew that the fake pond only existed because of an *Acceptance of Fakeness,* and these ducks were stuck in there with their real, made-by-nature wet undersides, and their faces and beaks and eyes, and then some idiot (me) who is *on drugs,* says that these ducks are not enough for her. As if they asked for me to assess their worth! It is simply the worst when I think of this moment, every time.

There were an estimated four sips left in the coffee cup, and this line of thought was really stressing me out, but still, I went for it and imagined An Exhausted Duck. I sat in the bed and I imagined a duck who was fed up with it all. The duck was fed up with being looked at by idiots who are lazy. The duck was saying with a stare, "You created this system, trapped me in it, you stare at me constantly and make sure I don't get out, and then you repeatedly say I'm not much at all! I was actually fine when

I was just free-ranging out there, and actually I was awesome, following ancient instincts and doing it perfectly. You are the ones who deserve to live in a replication of your natural environment, not me! You are the ones who have separated yourselves from all of your instincts and instead are constantly jerking off the reward sector in your dying brains. You are the ones who have few deep rhythms left, only needs and greeds and tiny, excruciating reactions to having your nerves pinged all the time by your ridiculous computer addictions. Hey, dickhead! How about I replicate *your* world and *you* see what *you* live in and how *you* are, with your fake deep 'farmhouse sinks' and your 'rain showers' and your library of a thousand or more pictures of yourselves that you keep on your murderous phones, you dicks! YOU WISH YOU COULD BE A MALLARD, YOU FUCK-ING SUCKERS!"

As I completed the final sip, my body was clenching because of the Exhausted Duck's monologue, and I exhaled a huge breath and released my muscles, and I thought that the whole thing about me being disappointed by the ducks was genuinely surprising, because ducks are actually in my top five maybe even top three of birds, along with sandpipers and egrets and the other seabirds. I set the mug down on the side table and then I made myself into the shape of a hook on the mattress, and I felt relief that I was sleeping on the correct side of my body, and then I fell back into sleeping.

I woke up from my brief extra sleep and I felt slightly upset because of all of the thoughts about animals and the zoo, and the phrase that I had thought of, "Acceptance of Fakeness," and how much it really burns me to be a part of a situation involving an Acceptance of Fakeness. I swept my touch like a wand over my fiancé's back and said that I would make the coffee, which is what I do every morning, but usually I just do it once.

I went into the kitchen and the dog clawed me basically to shreds in my nightgown, out of love. I put on the water and I put on the radio and listened about the plague, and I wrote down what I could remember of my dreams while the coffee was brewing, and then I came into the bedroom and set it all down and went to use the bathroom.

When I came back and we were having coffee, my fiancé said that Justin was probably hungry and that he felt bad about that. My baby will have a father who wonders if the trapped raccoon is hungry, and even "feels bad" about it. My baby will have a father who will not even kill a bug and is not afraid of a bug, but has the right amount of wariness and respect for a raccoon. He was not just trying to trick Justin into the trap, and he will not punish him for being there. He simply knows that we cannot live here together as a group. It does not work, and he is being direct about it. He has deep empathy for the times when we get stuck in the wrong place because we thought we wanted something that was not worth it. He understands what it feels like to be mistaken, and then resoundingly but temporarily stumped. He will only give Justin an interesting breakfast and guide him back to the right place for his wildness.

My fiancé went out and just a few moments later I observed

him through the bedroom windows, walking down the long dock in small quick steps and trying to carry the trap so that it was parallel with the dock, but the trap kept dipping because of Justin's weight, and I think I saw Justin looking out the back. My fiancé's plan was to take Justin in the boat over to the state park. It was the morning and he was taking the raccoon on a boat ride, something most raccoons will never achieve or enjoy. He was like the ferryman from one world to the next, from *temporary nightmare* to *totally fine.* I think I am fortunate to have a partner who will take a raccoon in a boat, calmly, to a place on the other side, and then come back here to me. There are so many different types of living things intersecting with each other, in troublesome encounters and in respectful ones. Many opportunities for setting things right, when you think about it. I thought about the houseguest and that I wished that I would not have to ask him about cleaning up his own small hot wet bags, but that I would, because I should learn to tolerate possibly being disliked by someone who does not totally understand me. I cannot make everything perfect but I can work on my side of the problem, like how my fiancé can't stop Justin from wanting to come to our trash, but he can orchestrate the outcome so that we don't have to live together in a way that is unbearable. To work on your side of the problem is to eradicate the Acceptance of Fakeness, at least for yourself. That is very refreshing to know!

And maybe I will do something else with my rage about the small hot wet bags. I thought that maybe I would find a nice area in my creative work in which to place the rage, somewhere where it couldn't cause any real damage, like maybe in a play about people in the past? I liked thinking about how even something unwanted (my uncomfortable rage) can still offer a weird doorway to something new in one's work. And so for that, I was thankful to our houseguest. And then I thought that the way that I will redeem myself with the ducks is that one day I will take my child to a real pond where some ducks are living in real nature, and I thought then that the child and I will be so glad to be there, and we will stay in our appropriate place on the shore of the pond, and we will toss many delicious morsels to the mallards, we will loudly marvel at them, and we will tell each other facts about them, and then we will collect any trash that we might have created, and we will thank the ducks for the visit, and we will leave them in peace. I felt wonderful about this whole plan, and perfectly amiable toward the houseguest, who ended up sleeping through most of the morning.

Excerpt 1 from the Play *Schumacher*

LETTIE Schumacher bustles up the front walk of a well-kept Victorian home. She can hardly untie her bonnet and stow her basket, she is so excited. She enters the parlor, where her parents are having a sherry. Her parents look up as she darts between them before landing at the piano. They are all wearing old-fashioned clothes and are old-fashioned, like in Meet Me in St. Louis.

LETTIE:

Oh you just won't *believe* it, I say, you just *won't*! Mama, Papa! Well, I hate to have to say it, I really do hate to be the one to break the news, and it's just so very shocking, but it seems that...well, it seems that everyone who was ever cruel to me has fallen into a very large hole! Have you heard? Oh, Mama, isn't it simply bizarre? Because how could they *all* fall? All of them at once! (*Her parents watch as she walks toward the window and murmurs dreamily.*)

One consolidated pouring of themselves, a pouring motion of all of those cruel people, just like rice from a clear glass jar. (*She turns back to her parents, who are watching her with light amusement. She speaks to them but also seems to be doing a calculation in her mind.*)

And right to the bottom of the hole! And you know, they were all together, walking as one horde. And to be quite honest it does chill me because it was so flawless how they...how it worked that they... (*She is reenacting it now, marking the spots and doing slight impressions of people*)...They all were walking together as one big horde, including that terrible employer I had, and of course those three brothers who were so fresh to me last autumn, you know, Mama? That fellow called Lud Roberts, and his brothers Derry and Tank, and they and all of the others were walking...like this...in a trance a bit, like with the blank faces that people have when...from the...a...well, who could ever say, but...perhaps because of a successful incantation that made them appear this way, but who could ever prove that? Right, Mama? And then there was suddenly a big dark hole in front of them and nobody shouted to the others to stop and nobody even stopped

themselves, really, and they all just tipped right in at the top
and then...then they fell down straight to the very bottom,
without any stopping until they hit.

*LAIRD enters. He is a teenager in old-fashioned tennis clothes and
a flat brimmed hat.*

LETTIE:
Oh, hello, Laird! How was tennis? Any luck?...Did you hear
about how all of the people who were cruel to me fell into
my...the...a...hole?

*LAIRD rolls his eyes but otherwise does not formally acknowledge
any of them, takes a very large crystal bowl of chocolates from a
table, flops onto the chaise, sets the bowl on his lap, and lazily starts
eating.*

LETTIE:
But, Mama, isn't it queer what intensity is in the air? And
think of *all of them*, think! All of them. All. Just down at the
bottom of an extremely large hole that is a perfect circle in
the road and they're just down there looking up. They are
not dead, *nobody said that!* They are not even hurt, thank
goodness! I do hear that they hit so hard that they won't ever
speak again, though. I do hear they have to be quiet forever,
and they just have to stand down there and look up to where

the rest of us will erect a corral around the hole and stroll around it. I hear that.

LAIRD plods out of the room and up the fancy stairs.

LETTIE:

Oh, Laird? Laird? Laird! Don't you *dare* lock that bathroom door! I was to be next for the bath, after Grandfather! Oh, Papa, *do* something! He's just *wretched*! He'll use up all the hot water and then what will I do about the Iced-Cream Social tonight? Oh, Papa, please! *Oh that fucking Laird!* I'm going to make it so that he scorches his penile off in that bathwater that he's so keen on! Oh, he's just beastly! (*Plainly, looking toward the place where the wall meets the ceiling*) He'll die.

LETTIE returns the crystal bowl of chocolates to where it was.

LETTIE:

There, Mama, your chocolates. Anyhow, the hole and all that... it is certainly an unfortunate turn of events. (*Smirking*) One of those things, I suppose.

MR. SCHUMACHER gets up from his chair, looks to the second floor, and heads up the stairs, presumably to deal with LAIRD, but of course we will never know. LETTIE drifts to the window and gazes out, dreamy once again. She fingers the fringe of the lace curtain and speaks in an increasingly absent-minded fashion.

LETTIE:
They are down there even now. It is really... such a shock. I bet I will think about it for quite a while, or at least while I am having my cocktail... after my bath. But at the Iced-Cream Social I shall devote all my attentions to the events of the evening. We've been waiting so long, it would be a shame to spoil it all by letting one's mind wander, don't you agree, Mama?

MRS. SCHUMACHER smiles calmly in agreement. She gets up from her seat, walks to the crystal bowl of chocolates and takes two, then pours a sherry for herself and a new one for her daughter, then crosses the room to bring LETTIE the drink and the candy, joining her at the window. They look out silently, threading their arms around each other's corseted waists.

Stork Dream: Smash

Some nights I dream of my Stork descending to the front door, a perfect landing, and the Stork is silent and proud, and I am washed and dressed and ready with the correct, innate arm control to just casually pick up my baby as if I know what to do. But sometimes I am stricken by a terrible dream of the Stork being late, and then descending too fast, and bursting into flames. Feathers and flesh being cooked, a moment of flames and floundering and the terrible bird-screech of a billion-year-old deity ending in disaster, and then just a dropping item that I can see falling from so far up there, from so high I see the dropping of bird-leg bones and talons and burning feathers, and there is no noise until the sound of the impact with the ground, and then there is no noise after that, because I never speak again or move or exist.

Is it a premonition, or just a flare of fear? What is the message? Is there some violence that I don't understand? I admit it, I do not have easy faith in the process, and I am so frightened that something will be wrong, and I think it is not irrational to be frightened. Yesterday morning I was in the middle of the living room, doing my squatting-down and leg-lifting. Outside, the wind was absolutely whipping, and the trees were bending in shocking contortions. Then last night I dreamed that I was back in the living room, lifting and squatting and looking at the storm outside, and in the dream I thought, *What if it is like this outside when the Stork is trying to bring the baby? It is already so hard to believe that such a wicker-like being could hold the weight of a baby, although I do seem to know that the beaks are very strong, fearsome even.* And there was a part of me that was tossing and turning my own beached body in the bed, trying to wake up, telling myself to stop the story, but I couldn't help dropping my mind farther into the dream: The Stork is in the gale, and then is huffed right out of the sky, and then spit down, and battered against some cliffs, mercilessly creamed against big rocks, and my baby slipping into the sea like a bar of soap.

Even when I woke up and took a sip of water and reoriented myself and put the big pillow between my thighs to help with my back pain, even when I really reset myself, I still went back into the dream and the terrible things that happen to the Stork kept presenting in my mind: its broken legs, a swollen-shut eye and one rolling eye, wings snapped and soft parts pulped, like paste and straw. I saw it: the body of the bird totally trounced, like how a cheap umbrella gets slapped inside out and the flimsy wires just give out, poke out, bend and twist. In my dream I turned my head away from the view of the rocks and I saw the old TV from my grandmother's house. It had the big knobs on it and there was a broadcast of a cooking show, but the chef was just lowering gigantic objects into the pot, like a houseplant and a pair of figure skates, like how Mary Poppins unpacks, but in reverse? The chef was way too out of breath to have her own show, and she was explaining, "A lot of Stork-waiters have fantasies or wishes that they are sharing a Stork with their best friend or someone like that, but in most cases, you are sharing your Stork with a stranger, and so this is also a great opportunity for personal growth, ladies!"

I woke up and my heart was pounding like the fist of a hand of someone locked in a room. I am afraid of what will happen to my body in the birth, that must be what this Stork thing is really about. Those are the parts of the dream that I understand and also dread. I don't understand the 1980s TV and the chef, but I do understand why you would hope to share your Stork with someone who loves you, or why you would hope for some way to not feel so alone. But in the waking world, even if your best friend birthed their baby in a bed right next to you, even if you have a partner who would do anything for you and they are holding your hand, they still cannot be your body. And they still cannot be inside of you. Only the lifeform is inside of you, and it has to come out, and there is an essential aloneness in that task that cannot be reconfigured. And this is not necessarily a bad thing even while being a frightening thing, and it must be met, and is living in my dreams, and is also real.

Seal Scales

The day was one of those precious ones where the air is all cloud, even down here on the ground, and there are cycles of rains, and you really get a sense of the drops as they come down. I spent my morning talking on the telephone, and I also organized and put into baskets all of my usable underwear and socks and slips and bras. I spoke on the phone with my best friend as I picked out underwear and bras that were now too small because my stomach and breasts are larger at this point in the pregnancy, and my hips are holding more too, and so I decided to mail my underpants and bras to myself in the future, and I put them in a sack to put in a box and put in the mail. One of my best qualities is whimsy combined with being sensible and acting on that sensibility right away, but on behalf of the whimsy, to help it work. Whimsy cannot whirl itself through cluttered and junked-up spaces. Whimsy is not the same as kookiness and it is the opposite of laziness.

I spent the afternoon alone, eating snacks and a half of a donut, plus reading, and moving through the house for this or that, and going to the bathroom. My fiancé had gone to his mother's house to have a long talk and a walk with her, and I stayed here with the donut and the dog.

In the late afternoon he returned and we sat at the kitchen table, and we each had a glass of water, and he told me about his conversation with his mother, who we all love and are very interested in. I had taken off my underpants while we were in the kitchen, explaining that they were too small for me now, and then I placed them on the table while we kept talking. I felt that the underpants were listening to us. I made a note to put them with the other intimates that were already in the sack in the box to be put in the mail to myself in the future.

We moved ourselves to the living room to do some work, but I decided to do a prank. The prank was that I walked gracefully toward the middle of the carpet and did sort of a fake ballet move but then I sniffed the air like an animal and I pretended to be a changeling, and then I pulled up my dress and growled and squatted and flashed him my vagina, because I thought it was funny to be a wild-pregnant-mammal-thing. My fiancé had a shocked look when I did my prank, and right as I did it I felt a weird feeling, like the tilt of a situation when you realize that there is something extra there, like another set of eyes. When I moved my eyes to where my guts told them to move, I saw that he was not so shocked by my prank, but concerned because our front garden and the large rock and unfinished bridge next to our house were positively overrun by children, at least five little boys, plus a baby girl with a blond round head. When I went to the kitchen door to peek out and say that they should be careful because the bridge was not completed, I saw my fiancé's cousin standing at the picket fence in her yellow rain jacket, which made me think that maybe she *did* see my prank but it was not worth it at all to ever look into that. She asked us if we had seen the baby seal that was by the dock. It is more than rare to see a seal by our dock, but it can happen, because the dock is at the meeting point of the river and the ocean. Of course we went right down to see it, and we brought binoculars and went into the boat and motored gently toward where the baby seal was in the water. There, a little bit into the water, was a baby pup putting its head up like a darling ocean-dog, and also it felt like an omen, this baby animal waiting for us, lingering, and looking right at us. And when I thought to myself that it was like an omen, I saw the image of the lifeform inside of me looking right at the baby seal, and I posited that they could certainly see each other, because the lifeform inside of me—while it is attaching to its human life and sipping in portions of its spirit every day—is of course able to gaze right into the eyes of anything "baby" or anything "ancient" that is on this planet and close to the seams of the other dimensions, very new or very old.

It did not feel unsettling to think this, it felt normal, like making a small smile, or squinting to keep your best sight while faced with a bright light.

After watching the baby seal for a short while, we decided to go farther out onto the ocean, and we went rather fast, and right toward where the terns were diving and the bluefish were flinging themselves into the air from the surface of the water. I had no shoes on, as I had rushed down to the dock to see the seal pup. I put my bare feet down on the floor of the boat and I stood very sturdily and with the eyes of my little lifeform looking out from inside of me, I cast that line out into the activity. We caught the bluefish on the line and it pulled so that the line was an arch, and it pulled for its life, and I felt that freaked-out, frantic tug, and I was scared to have won. But we pulled it in, and my fiancé did the rest, which I do not want to discuss because it involved bonking the fish right on its head while it slammed itself in desperation on the bottom of our boat.

The fish had a sheen of violet on its scales, and when we returned to the dock the baby seal was there, and it was periscoping right at us with its round globes of black eyes and smooth head, and it looked into the lifeform in my body and then it did another thing: It looked right up at the sky and just kept looking up into it, like how you might look directly up if, by mistake, you walk in on someone changing. And that was not the wrong way to look at me because I am currently really changing.

When we got off of the dock, my fiancé asked me to go get a

long sharp knife and a big plate for the fish, plus bug spray for us. You have to clean the fish on the dock because it is too messy for inside, even though I said *Let's just do it in the sink* because I did not understand.

He showed me how to do it: First you scrape off the scales, and you hose them off the dock and away from the body of the killed fish so that you do not get scales in your dinner, and the scales flush right back into the water, but without the fish that they were once a part of. Then you put the fish down on the boards of the dock and you make three connected slits as a boundary between the gill and the body of the fish and then you cut along the underneath line, and at that point, you can see and talk about the guts and fish parts. Then you make two more cuts, one above the tail and one along the top ridge of the fish, and unzip the big part that we call the fillet. There is not as much blood as you think, and it is not bright red like ours, but in fact more the color of a jam or blueberry juice.

As he was cutting, I noticed how calm and capable he is, and how intelligent to remember these exact moves that he must have learned so long before now. Then I thought about when I met him in Norway. I had been bending over to look at something at a horse farm, who knows what. He was standing behind me, but then he also bent to try to see, and he was close to the side of my neck and I heard him smell me, and I *knew* that he did it. There are times when you do not decide to either remember or to forget, but it is more like the event goes right into your blood, to always be returned to your heart again and again, cleaned and returned, again and again. Or maybe the perfect moment becomes a perfect shape, a round bone in the vertical collection that makes up your spirit-spine. But what person being smelled in their hair and neck while leaning over at a Norwegian horse farm could ever know that this was what was really happening?

I did look down at the round of my body, rounding out underneath the dress I wore, and I indulged in my game that I sometimes do: I see in my mind that he is in Norway in the past and he smells my neck and hair like he did. I start with what happened, but then I make it that when he smells me, he gets carried by a kind of huge tidal-breath into his future, and much like how we observe our lives or our own selves in dreams, just set aside but perfectly flush with the moment, he sees himself teaching me how to cut up my fish that I caught, and I see myself as he sees me: that I am a good listener, and I have the lifeform there under the dress, in me, because we have had sex together in his very bed! And he watches from his moment of cosmic access as I squat down to say what I see about the dark color of the fish blood on this dock with this dead violet fish in pieces, scales scattered in the wind and then into the water. In my game I imagine one mind-blowing moment where he smells me and is granted that peek at a version of the future and he realizes, "She is my wife!" This is my absolute favorite part of the game and it does a lot for me every time I play it.

When we came inside I made a phone call but it was not raining anymore like it was during my phone calls earlier in the day. I called the airline and asked them some questions in regard to my travel and the plague and what is happening on the planes and in the airports. While I was doing this, he cooked us the fillets that he sliced from the fish. When I was done with the phone, the fish was cooked and already on a long plate on the table plus there were candles, and we ate it with some pleasure but a little fear because, when it comes down to it, we killed this thing, didn't we?

And what happened then was that he got up to watch the sun go down over the marsh and river. It set itself down behind the tree line on the other side of the water. At first, I was too hungry to watch another sunset, and I just wanted bread, and to sit, but he said *Let's sit outside to watch it,* even though the sun had left already and the sky was just colors without the orb. As we sat, the clouds above the water seemed to get brighter, and I said it was as if the sun was about to come back up, and the clouds held the light in an illuminated seam, like it could crack and drip the light down onto the trees. The clouds held color, but their form was also like a sort of breathing. We both did say that something felt different, and then I knew what it was, but for a moment I was afraid to say it. When you see and feel something extraordinary, but you see it privately, it can still be complete and real for you. If you tell another person, though, maybe the other will not agree, or worse, they will not see it, and then the whole thing can collapse onto itself. But what is the point of being truly close to someone if you are afraid to tell them what you are realizing?

So I said, "If you look level at the sky, you can see that the sky behind the tree line is not the sky, but it is actually a *secret sea* that is revealing itself, and that the dark gray clouds there are *actually* land masses and islands." He asked a few good questions, mostly about where to look, simple requests for directions and ways to orient himself, and then he saw what I was saying, and then we both started to see more.

I saw that what I thought were clouds holding the seam of light was actually a golden coast. And we saw the sky as a further sea, and as the breath of pinkish clouds at the top of the image revealed more and more of the "sky sea," we felt it was real, and that the scrim between worlds was being lifted for us just for this moment. And he said something about how *it let us see it because we are patient* and I agreed, and I loved him for understanding things like this. We spoke about the whole event in a whisper.

Then we saw his aunt and uncle walking down the dock in these long shorts and button-up shirts, and their dog was jutting ahead of them, and I said, "Isn't it funny that Vicky and Bob cannot see the thing that we are seeing right now, even though it is what we are all looking at?" I thought to call down to them and invite them up and point it all out, but that did not feel appropriate in the end. And he asked me *Should we say thank you for showing us?* And I said yes, and so he out-loud thanked the world that had revealed itself, and I said *Thank you* in my head so that the lifeform could hear it in herself too, and he asked me *Did you know that you just kissed the air?* And then he and I also kissed. Then he said that he would go put the chickens to bed, which made me love him but also caused a pinprick of jealousy because I think those chickens don't like me. I guess you can't have everything.

And now it is dark. There is a rich peace that soaks into the ground after it has enjoyed a day of drinking in the raindrops slowly. Tonight, after a day of rain, the humid air is thrumming with the chimes and high creaks of bug noises, those small cranks and dingers and whistles under the stars. From the bed, I observe the night. I can only see what the darkness offers, but I know that a little baby seal slips through the water, that she sees the moon as a wavy light from under the water, and as she glides on her back and looks at the light, she lets fall onto her tongue the violet scales of the fish that is now inside all of us.

Raccoon Gossip

What he said to her is that "the guy there is a total freak, but not a bad one," and that all you need to do is "go there when you feel the normal feeling that comes in the night," and that "basically you can do your own thing, like, there's not a window of time to get it right," and he just kept saying that he swears that "nothing is going to happen to you."

Apparently he had been going over there since around the end of the winter, when you can feel that thing in the ground, underneath your paws, and sometimes you feel it shushing through your fur. He had been going since around that time of year, and he felt that it was a normal area, but maybe better than normal, because there were so few Spikes of Warning, and so

few of the Spikes of potential violence and death, the invisible
Spikes that you can feel jolting up around you when you are like,
"I want to go over here, but I can tell that I might die." We knew
a groundhog who didn't listen to his Spikes, and he didn't die,
but he got bonked on the head by a shovel, and then he couldn't
hear anything ever again, and then of course did die, because we
all do, but that was from something else. He fell, I think.

I've always felt that it wasn't worth it for him, like, whatever
he was trying to get? There is no way that whatever he wanted
was worth hearing literally nothing forever, like it's not like there
was a bucket of oatmeal or spaghetti where he'd been. That was
the weirdest part, like, why was he even where he was? It was
an old garden with not even any lettuce or beans, just raspberry
bushes and chives and it's just like, "Maybe that groundhog got
bonked because he was already stupid?"

But either way, what Justin told her was that he'd been going
up there since that time in the end of the winter and that it had
been normal, and that he had made a crashing noise by mistake,
but then he didn't see any new light or hear anything coming, so
he picked around, and then drank from a can of pineapples, and
he got juice and a few pieces of the fruit, and when he looked up
from the can, he saw two of them looking at him from the door,
but he said (and honestly it might just be bragging) that he *knew,*
like he just knew that they weren't going to do anything, but that
then he left because the can was over and there *were* a few Spikes
coming up for him, and, "For me, if I have more than three Spikes
coming up, especially if the can is over, it's not worth it."

And then he said he just kind of kept checking it out, and usually there was nothing because they keep the trash inside the place, but then their opening was broken, or they forgot to close it, and so he got into it, and he got lots of stuff, even coleslaw, apparently.

And then he said that he went there one night and the *whole thing* was open, and so he went all the way in, and he even went up and into the big space. He said that's when the guy came out with only skin on and small white shorts, and he had a dog who was going totally crazy, like she was totally overstimulated by Justin being there? And even though she had no idea how to handle herself and wasn't even chasing him but was just going all over the place, nothing but impulses ricocheting around randomly, he said he was still scared and had a lot of Spikes so he climbed up on top of the window, and I guess the dog just went somewhere else and pissed, and then went to the other side of the big space and took a whole shit in the stone thing with the burned up logs in it.

Then he said this guy just started laying out all of these squares of cheese, leading to the opening to the big thing, like leading back to the outside, not further in, and that then the guy kind of backed out and backed away, like farther into the big thing? So then Justin said he thought that it *was* actually super weird, like something was off, and that even though he actually should have had *more* Spikes than he had, he still left and didn't take the cheese. He weirdly also decided to randomly shit all over the place right before he left, which he didn't try to explain and kind of glossed over when he was telling her. She said it was like he wanted her to know and couldn't keep it to himself, but he also didn't seem to have the introspection to be able to really say *why* he did it. But from what she understood, it was not like *in response* to the shit that the dog made while freaking out. It wasn't meant to goad her. And then he said he was like, "Nooooo, I *should've* taken that cheese," and so he came back, but he was loud by mistake again, and then the guy came back, and he thought maybe the dog was about to come too, so then he was like, "Actually this *isn't* worth it," and he left again.

Even though the area and place had the guy, and his confusing cheese, and his strange dog, Justin still felt drawn to the place, and so when the feeling came when it normally comes, he picked that place again, and this time when he got there, he saw the metal thing next to the trash. At the back of it was half of a banana and some cornbread, just sitting there. And he said that he did get a few Spikes, but that bananas give him super bad judgment and he was like, "This *is* worth it. This is *everything to me right now.*" And so he walked in, and the second he got to the back, the front opening slammed and now it was a Closed Thing. And there he was. And he was honest about it that it was terrifying. You know how it feels bad to be where you don't want to be as the night ends and the day comes back around, like how it feels really loud even though it isn't, and the air feels wrong, like there's not enough soil in the air, like morning air is water being combed with dusts of light, and night air is like soil and moon-strokes? He felt that disgustingly real fear of being in the wrong air, and he was like, "Oh, I actually might die here."

He said of course he had no choice. He had to be there, so he ate the cornbread and the banana and he said that it was really good, not like trash, or with something on it that you have to "work with," like no plastic on the food, or mold or anything. And then the guy came and Justin was like, "Am I going to die?" But then the guy gave him a half a donut, and Justin said, "So then I was like *truly* what the fuck?" And the guy started to carry him, *in the metal thing,* down the dock and to the water and that then Justin really did just go crazy in there because he was like, "This fucking guy is gonna dump me in this water and I'm gonna go all the way down and I'm gonna die!"

Instead, the guy takes Justin onto a boat. And he takes him across the river to that forest there, and he just lets him out, and that was it. And that was really it. He didn't hurt him at all or do anything weird or try to keep him, and he didn't do anything bad at all. Justin was like, "This fucking guy only does good?" And just to test it, the next night Justin went back and the same thing happened again, except he got different things to eat (quesadilla), and the guy was better at carrying the thing down the dock, like he was smoother at it.

She said he invited her and said to her over and over again that nothing bad was going to happen, and she had a few Spikes come up about it but she decided to go, and they went, and the only thing was that it was crowded in the metal thing with both of them in it, but that also she *did* like it, and she *was* scared, but ultimately they were safe. And so now we all know: "This guy's a total freak! He just likes to give you a meal and then take you for a ride."

I think that what she got was grapes and tuna and I'm not sure but I actually think they each had crackers too.

And I haven't tried it yet because nobody has invited me, but also maybe I will just go alone. Because for me, I want the experience, but I want it *least* for the meal. And second least for the ride, which I am slightly more interested in because I have never ridden in a boat. But mostly I want to do it to test how it will feel to be unable to move and really have to deal with that, like, to tolerate it as I watch the night end and the morning rise up so loudly in front of me. Knowing that I will be freed shortly, and that all of my freedom and the rest of my life is out there? I think it might be useful to me to feel the very size of my real wildness rise inside. Who really knows what I will do with any information that I get, but perhaps if I can watch calmly as my most innate parts react to the temporary truth that my body has been apprehended, I will see what really comes up, and I then can explore its uses once I am free again. I just want to see who I'd be when that happens. I want to see what I'm like when I face it.

Vision of Water Column

In the vision, I was sitting up in the bed and looking at the water. I looked through air and then glass and then through more air, and then my sight landed down on the long grasses, and the water, and the paste of silt, and the density beneath. When I saw the water washing through the marshes outside our window, I suctioned my tongue to my top palate and I thought, *This is an Act of Marsh,* an Act of Marsh within me. I tasted the dirt and salt, and in my mind-mouth I swished around the fish-flickers and the crab-worries. I was looking into the marsh, thinking: So much living and life happening, and a lifeform in my belly, and the grasses and rushes and the whole living collection. Do you believe me when I say that the water itself knew that I knew all about it? The water knew, *A nearby mammal is making a lifeform inside of itself, and inside of itself it makes new body parts, little sacks, new drinks, and chemicals and hallways and little bones.* The water knew that I knew about having a lot of living and changing going on within me. The water said, "She is a lot like me."

The water is about fullness, and it is about draining out, and it is about revealing what is underneath. The tides are about total depth and then total bareness, and you cannot ever stop them from always being concerned and involved with both of those things. The water is about bulging in exaltation of the fullest, closest moon, and then pulling together and away when that moon is not near to its beloved, which is the water. And I, with my lifeform in my own self-made inside-sea, knew all about the fullness, and I anticipated the eventual emptying of the marsh.

In the vision (because the water knew that *I knew*), the marsh filled with the wanting of me, and of the little lifeform in me, as if we were its personal moon. It gathered itself up, building up and flowing in toward itself, and I saw a new type of tide: The water stood itself up in the marsh, all of the water stood itself up into one column, making the dock naked, baring the soft floor of the marsh itself, showing me everything. The lowest tide ever occurred, what I called a "Naked Tide" in my head as I watched the water stand itself up.

The underneath was revealed and wet, and wanting to do suction to anything that would touch it. All of the water that had been lapping at the pilings and the wooden floats was gathered up in a perfect vertical pillar, a waterfall attached to nothing, water falling and ascending at once like a timer, like a guardian, like a mirror of two heartbeats: mother-beat on top, baby-beat below.

The two players were the upright water and me, the woman with the lifeform inside of her. In the vision, this newly formed column, this water-entity, charged me up as I held it in my gaze. The more I looked at it, the more power I made inside of myself, and I sent it all down to the hold where the lifeform flipped around. The column of water made me bold and it made me want to double down on this period of transformation. I was suddenly gung ho about my commitment to transform until I geysered something new out of myself. So what did I do? I opened my mouth with a wicked-wide smile, and it was like when they hold the flag up at the start of the car races. But those cars are filled with mostly men, and they only go in a dusty circle.

Flag down.

The water rotated its whole form from vertical to horizontal and closed the distance between the outside and the bedroom. It flew at me like a damn witch on her live broom! The beam of water spared me nothing as it slammed into my open face. Pregnancy is about transformation, but some of it is so unexpected, for example, the top of my head hung open at the jaw, my skull cleanly split exactly across its equator so that I was two bowls, conjoined. The water had slammed me apart and then it kept coming in and in and in. The marsh water, brackish, smuggling ocean water in itself, thick with phosphorescent creatures, that water dove to find the little lifeform down inside.

The water went down, and it explained to me as it descended, "I and these salts and minerals and glowing creatures that are in me, we are flowing down to the lifeform, and we are breaking your head now so that nothing intense or fractured or normally impossible will seem alien to you ever again. The weirdness, the thing that one might say could never occur, it will occur, in a pattern of events that even I, the ancient water who started everything, cannot predict or control. But we are here now to help you get ready for the unknowable, for the most precious endowment and the most confounding changes. Everything must break, everything must split open. What is usually a sign of an emergency has shifted slightly over into a different definition. What will occur lives on the blade-line between total emergency and the life-springing, everyday work of a deity. It will be you who sees it all and is all of it."

When my mind released me from this vision, I could hardly get to the toilet in time. And all day long I drank in more and more water. All day long I felt that I had the finest posture I had ever been able to produce in this skeletal frame. I was a perfect column, straight up and down, and the top of my head felt simple and light, like an overturned clean empty bowl made of bone and energy, and the lifeform inside of me flipped like a fish, and my perceptions seemed to be flooding in and coming from everywhere.

The Quake

Right before the birth, there was an earthquake at our house in Massachusetts. The center of the trembling was located in the water just off of the land where our house is. But we were in California, and so we did not feel a thing, at first. We had returned to California to do the birth, because even though the plague was happening and nobody had any major solutions yet, and even though we could only see our friends from many feet away, I wanted to be near them once the baby was with us. I would still have physically come apart, but they would be so close around me that I would not shake to pieces in the aftermath of the event. They would make it easier to stop being shook up. They would be a soft cushion of people.

The person house-sitting our house in Massachusetts told us about the quake. She wondered about the stability of the dark wooden chandeliers in the house. She said they swung around. They have been up there since someone in my fiancé's family put them up there one hundred years ago when they built this house to be a party hall for guests from Boston.

Maybe the earth shifted when we left, like finally waiting to scratch a deep itch once you are alone.

The quake seemed to me to be a signal that my baby would arrive soon, that the first push had come from its ancestral home on the other side of the country. I did think it possible that I might get a sign that would be from outside of my body. I assumed it would be from the sky, because it is my natural inclination to look up for guidance. I was frightened by what was to come. It is like letting the gods revel or do an intense ceremony in your own form. You have to be strong enough to hold the structure for them, to not let it kill you, and to let them do their thing in the full way that they need to do it.

The first sign came from the water. A necessary, involuntary shifting deep beneath. And then I started to get the messages in my own body, big moves beginning. When the baby was starting to come, we had asked the friend who was at our house in Massachusetts if there was any damage. She said that what had happened was frightening, that she had feared for the house, but after all of the jolts, nothing was a disaster. I was on my way to let this thing happen to me, and we were driving to the hospital in the city where my friends were all around. I was thinking about how the new buildings are made so that they can bend when the ground beneath them moves in unthinkable, seemingly impossible waves. There are so many ways to shore yourself up, and one of them is to be flexible during intensity. I checked the message from our friend who was watching our house. She was telling us more details of what happened in the quake, and she said that after it was all over, the house was still there and it had been shaken but it was still the house, and that all around it, the water was so clear.

Birth Visualization of Stone House

Downstairs, sitting on a couch and in an armchair, and often reaching to the coffee table for crackers and cheese and clusters of light green grapes, are my dead grandfathers. They are socializing with each other, one tall, generous, and confident, one small and shy but sturdy, too.

My great-grandmother, who is my father's grandmother, is going in and out, not a lot, just *in* sometimes to get napkins or to see about the coffeepot, and then *out*. And she looks out the kitchen window, and when in the living room, she looks up the stairs to where I am, in our bedroom, in the whirlpool of leaves, colors, shells, petals, and condensation that has formed around me because it is time for the lifeform to be born.

Lifeform

All of the people who love me, all of my family who have loved me, have never left me. They gather from their other dimensions, and they make a small family party. They prepare all of the food and they do all of the talking. They are not visiting, they have descended into a place that exists as a perpetual home for anyone in our family ever. We come here to be born, to give birth, to die, and then when we are dead we attend all events. All of my dead relatives proclaim, with their presence here, that we are an unbroken group. And they say, "We have always been loving you and we have never left you."

My grandmother Rochelle, my father's mother, the newest of the dead, is in the kitchen, sitting at the table. She loves to be with her mother. Believe it or not she has a cigarette and a cup of coffee. On the other side of the table is her father, and he is smoking, too. They have all been through this before: The children of the family have grown up and are now bringing in new lifeforms. They are pleased, they know what to do, they have full confidence in me and in their gathering.

I can hear all of their voices and I understand the different languages that they speak. I can feel how much they love their crackers and drinks and the cheese. I love how they all get along, and I love that they are truly mine. This has always been one of my favorite setups: Beloveds downstairs while I am upstairs and I can hear them, but I am taking some time for myself. Sometimes I would do this at the Seder. I would leave and go upstairs to my room but I would not ever be gone.

Within a gathering whirlpool of leaves, colors, shells, petals,

127

and condensation, I am upstairs in my bed. While I still share my body with the lifeform, and I still share my bloodstream with her, I pump the truth into her strong, new mind. I say, "I am your mother and everyone in my family who has ever loved me has never left me, even in death, and just like those who have gathered to help you come in, I will never leave you and I will always love you. You are from me and you will never be left out of my love, ever."

As I say this to the lifeform, and she hangs upside down inside of me, she opens her little mouth and drinks to this love, and she feels this truth on her brow, like perceiving sunlight through closed lids. When I tell the lifeform about our family, my grandfathers and my great-grandmother and my grandmother and my great-grandfather look up like they heard a bell ring, they look up the stairs to where we are, and they know that I have sent the message, and that everything is running on time and as it should. They look back at each other and make eye contact. They nod. And then it is time for me to make a temporary world for myself, for my comfort while coming apart.

On the day that my baby is born, I call a realm and it gathers itself in, to be used as a place that is just for this occurrence. I call it in after I have slept almost the whole night, after my brain has been washed clean by its primordial chemicals, after my psyche has done whatever blaring and questioning and protesting it needs to do in order to settle down and be of good use during the sunshine hours. Water gathers first while I am sleeping, in small happy teardrops that fill the bedroom. The whole space in my room that is usually air fills up with such small floats of water. And then the day's light comes too, and the darkness from the night lands down to form a dark blue soil all around the house, and green shoots grow up in it immediately, a billion blooms, and fat, shiny pumpkins, and fans of ferns, and the land around us is decorated by ponds and groves, orchards and houses and gardens blasting with lettuces, and melons bouncing on their vines, bold red tomatoes, and peas twirling up on their lattices. All colors of cows. All faces of sheep and their bells.

The Eternal Family House is an old, clean, rectangular stone house in a small hilly town. We are certainly not in any country you have ever heard of. In the country in the town where I am in the house with my beloved dead, the sun is very warm but never too hot. Nothing ever pounds here. The seasons go like this: an easy warm summer with long days that have early mornings, late sun-settings, green grasses that never crab or get browned, and flowers blooming throughout the whole time, even in winter. Here is where the house is: on the top of a hill and you can walk there from the center of the town, which is on the coast of the country.

In the town where I have my baby there is a graveyard with graves as old as they get, and dry skeletons in boxes or just in the ground, some turned to soil already, on their way to being magnetized into invisible matter and energy, an energy that knows everything, knows what to do with everything. The graveyard is also a garden with many benches and fountains, and all varietals of flowers that are made directly from some of the bones of the dead. Hard bones transition to silken blooms in only one dose of sunlight and one wash of moonlight. Everything in the realm that I make for the entrance of the lifeform, everything is connecting and changing at a quick, uninterrupted pace.

In the garden in the graveyard in the town in the country where I have my baby, there are geese and turtles there to gather with you. They have different personalities from normal geese or turtles because they are very friendly and solicitous. There is a dog who lives there, it knows you. It knows me. There are bugs but they are not scary or stingers. Honeybees have soft furry butts. There are many singing bugs like crickets, and many bugs for good luck and brief companionship. There are skunks but they save their spray. There are wolves and raccoons in the night but they share from the garbage cans and they all have enough. Nobody, no person or animal, would ever tear at another, not in the place where my lifeform starts her living. I will have to be the center of the violence, and it will be the only time that type of violence will occur for me, but it will be worth it, and I will be cared for by the people who are in attendance.

When the apple-shaped gland in my skull drips the chemical message through my body, I am in the kitchen in a nightgown and bathrobe, having my coffee and dipping toast strips into a soft-boiled egg. I am talking to my mother and my grandmothers and my great-grandmothers. I am with the living and I am with the dead. Everyone in my family who has ever loved me has never left me. They hear the drip of the gland like a sweet, tiny, painful ding, and they all walk with me up the stairs to my bed and they settle me in and then they retreat but they are not lost from me, they are just downstairs again.

Now the inside of my body is filled with plasma and soft light from the sun. The waves from the ocean that surrounds my town have lent me their rhythms and their many powers, some that science knows and some that only the universe itself has a language to tell about. I become stretchy and wide. All of the air comes in.

The water that filled the room has dissipated and now there is just a tiny bit of moisture in the air, there is no dust, there is only good comfortable warmth. The whirlpool of leaves, colors, shells, and petals falls to the floorboards and then lets itself out the window. I am pulling in so much that almost everything else needs to leave to give me more space. Because I hold the power of the waves, the sea outside is calm, yet still filled with whales and fish and turtles and the water surrounds me and my town and my house and my bed and my body and I pull in all of the power, keep pulling it in, and the pressure mounts as the power sends the chemical messages through my system, and I feel a deafening riot of fear. I feel a hugeness of pain, and loudness of pain, and I know that this was what was always going to happen to me but I am still dominated by how massive it is.

All of my beloved dead are downstairs in the living room and they are looking up to the bedroom. Each face is turned up. So much has gathered to be the help that I need when I become the center of an electric road, when I am hours of pain and will become a self-made moment of violence.

My beloveds are here to hold the beauty around me so that I can do this work which is over the top but not out of my league, because I am the one who has actually constructed all of this beauty, and I have also called in my beloved dead to gather in our Eternal Family House and then I made the realm around us. I have made this entire thing we are all in, I have made it with my mind, so that I can have the world I need, no matter where I am. I use my mind to consort with the clan that will help me find the courage to complete this work that I have done with my body for these many months. Even the lifeform's physical body was actually made with the power of my brain. I did not make my mind or its capabilities, and I hardly understand any of it, but I know that it is mine, and that I am led forward by the systems in me and by the mystery in me.

For many hours and through the night, I talk in screams to my ancestors downstairs, and I sleep and I yell and I vomit lightning into big bowls that my great-grandmothers occasionally toss out the windows and into the air, and so the storm in the sky is colossal at this point, but the sea is black and flat and reflects nothing. I look out the windows at my lightning, and at my husband, and we are there with each other, and everyone is there with me, and everything is with everything, and then it all lets go and my baby daughter, like a mini comet, rips into this start of her life, and it is violent and it is excruciating, but it is supposed to happen, and I am here still, and my husband is here, and all of my people are here, and the windows are open and the town is still there and the ocean is all around, and now the baby is here too.

The ocean welcomes back its waves. I am done with them now and I am relieved to detach from their strength. There is no more lightning, there are only constellations in the quiet sky, and the moon. The surface of the water wears the reflection of the lights that live in the sky. A certain effort is over now, and knowing this, my beloved dead all recline and relax and clink a glass downstairs. Everyone in my family who has ever loved me has never left me, and as I put my baby to my breast, and she takes her first drink of the life I have made for her, my ancestors take a restorative sip of their preferred cocktails. My beloved dead relax in the living room of our Eternal Family House, a domain that has welcomed me twice, once as a baby, once as a mother, and will finally host me one day too.

Phase 4: Baby

Letters to the Doctor: Crack Running Down?

Dear Doctor:

I haven't heard anything about the results of my tests but I am getting impatient and I am just wondering, from what you saw in the physical exam, do I have a crack running down from my dome to my flippers? From what I can see, there is a six-pounder stuck to my breast and also I am too hurt to push turds. Please let me know what the tests show, as I am trying to purchase clothes online and I can't choose things for myself because I don't even know what body coverings to buy and for what kind of body, even.

Love,
I'm not sure what to write here right now

The Great Conjunction

You were born out of me, one single time, during an astrological event that they called the Great Conjunction. At that time, everything in the sky and in the universe and all that exists was in a certain configuration, and so this is a part of your spiritual insignia.

Physically speaking, you were born out of me, and I am a mammal and I also have a soul. I am not an old soul like your father, who has dreams in which he can smell water on ancient stones, and feel the heaviness of his homemade armor as he lies injured within it, during another life that was also his, but before. Spiritually speaking, your father is strung with life-strings from hundreds of years ago, or a thousand, or a time before recorded time, but also the 1980s when his current body was born.

I am not an old soul at all. I think I may hold in me a new soul, very new, high-voiced, blinking into the light and trigger-happy, living in a "first" over and over again. As for the sky when I was born, there was a new moon in it, a brand-new moon, and so mark in me a reiterated newness. I am not a good dreamer like your father. I dream things like I am naked in front of the babysitter by mistake, or, "Oh no! I ate a mitten!," or I am fooled by a teenager, and I wake up with hurt feelings, but then I experience relief when I learn that I am in real life again.

When you were starting to be born, the doctor had to try everything to dislodge you from the opening of my vagina, and of course I had to try everything, too. I asked for them to put the needle in my spine so that I could not feel the pain anymore, but this also partially immobilized me, which was expected. In most cases, being immobilized from the waist down while having your whole vagina showing to a room of strangers would be an image from a fear-fantasy, but in this case, it was for health. The doctor, she had to try everything, and she was a very confident doctor who was respected and socially popular in the hospital, and so everyone was paying attention to what she might do to solve this problem of me having a baby Earthling stuck in the hole of my vagina during a notable astrological event. Eventually, she used a little plunger and stuck it to your small ball of a head, on the brand-new skin that I had *just* finished making for you to have on your head, and she pulled on that medical head-plunger with the force needed to end the clog, and some of the new skin on your head got ripped as she pulled, but then you were freed.

When you were born, I felt a bit timid around you because you seemed so self-possessed and so I did not want to intrude on you. They had taken you away from me, right away, because they realized that you had your total body but that you did not know how to use it. You were trying to learn to air-breathe, and they put you in a room full of other tiny strugglers. It was a few days before Christmas, and when I saw you again, you were wearing an incredibly small, striped stocking cap that they gave you to wear. It covered your cuts, and it was red and white for Christmas and you looked really good in it. You really did look like a baby elf, because of your smallness and your long striped stocking hat. Santa came and visited all of the babies in their clear incubators, and she was a woman with a big yarn beard and a red outfit over her nurse's outfit. Your spirit was settling into your tiny body like water running for the first time through a rill, and so as I said, I did not want to bother you.

Right after I grinded my pelvis open and split my very undercarriage to let you out and into your life, they took you away because you could not breathe, and I felt so ashamed that I did not know what was wrong and that I could not fix it myself, and that they had to take you *away* from me to fix you. I wanted it to be that you always *come* to me to fix things. Your father went with you because I could not walk yet. Neither you nor I could walk at all yet. I do not remember how I got out of where I was. I remember a hallway and that I could not see who was wheeling me toward where I was going. The loneliness in me felt metallic. I was a big empty bell clanging around looking for what I was supposed to be attached to. If the bell is not around the neck of its animal, the animal gets lost.

They brought me to a recovery room and I was trying to reassure myself that you were with your father, who had just become your father. I could not sense a recovery beginning in the recovery room. He sent me a picture of the two of you holding hands through the small plastic house that they had to put you in. I had met you for just enough time to tell you your name.

Once that first distance was closed and you left that room that had all of the other brave babies, and you came back to me after a few days, once I could begin my fussing and nursing and fulfill my mammal instincts, I realized how much we'd had to endure by being apart from each other like that.

I know that you will know me as the person who replaces the toilet paper and uses the vegetable peeler and is just spraying, spraying, spraying everything down. I say silent, shitty mantras, "This is all I do now. This is all I am." This morning I told your father that I have been absorbed into the same refrain that ate my mother and aunt: "My body hurts all of the time." Or sometimes I even say, "I think I am dumb now." I am aware that these clichés wait for the moments when I am unfocused and unprotected because of fatigue, and that they try to calcify self-criticism around me, so let me shake loose of that, and take you with me toward the truth of who I really am, even after exploding my vagina during something called the Great Conjunction.

I am your mother and you were born from me. I exploded my

vagina during a global plague, and during the astrological event called the Great Conjunction, a day after the winter solstice, an auspicious moment when the astrologers instructed us to start something new that we were willing to commit to.

I am a mammal with a soul made new every morning, and the first thing that I do is sniff the air, and then I sniff your father, and I turn my head toward your room that I made pretty for you, the walls patterned with fruit trees, and I sniff for you, too. Then I do the thing that you all think I do: pee. You guys think all I do is pee.

I saw you a few hours ago, just before dawn, when I nursed you and put you back to sleep. While you are still somehow asleep, I take this rare moment to choose mugs for coffee, "nice" the dog (for example, I put my forehead on the dog's forehead, give her compliments), put last night's dishes away, stand around looking, stand around looking, stand around looking, smell the smell of the coffee that I so cleverly set to brew while we were still asleep, stand looking, let the last of the sleepiness mist off, feel my feet pads push the wood on the floor, think about my nightgown, notice the temperature of my mouth, pour coffee into mugs.

I am also doing so much other work, besides the house and mother-work that I am always doing, which also sometimes seems hardly detectable.

I am the person saying, "This bread is moldy." But please take this as the more important fact: Because of the spirit-being that I am, I have consistently lived within a hive of purposeful pleasure. I hope this will be something that you know about me, and that you can depend on the fact that I will always pull you in with me to these happy hives, all sweet, no sting. Remember this about me? Perhaps it seems like I am dreary because of tiredness that has really washed me out. So much of being a new mammal mother, for me, is asking others to remember things about me that feel riptide'd out of my identity because I have become the manager of a teeny, busy hotel, and I have also morphed into the sheepdog in charge of an overwhelmingly important living parcel.

You are a baby and your brain changes so often and so majorly that it bucks you in your sleep, and you need me to come in and lift your small body up, and let the new parts of your brain know that they have arrived into the right lifetime, into the right body, and that yes they can live here because there is love here. I hold you in the dark and I keep imprinting on you that this is where the love is, that it will find you even in the dark, even if you have a new brain that you just made. I always know the signal, especially if it is new. That is my specialty, in fact.

Compared to you, I am much more used by life now, blasted through by many cycles, and in spite of an essential feeling of newness in my spirit, things have established themselves in the halls of my mind. It's an absurd, cacophonous scene in there. Haughty Old Belief-Beings, stressed out on their thrones, Beggars and Clowns, supine and drooling on the marble, huge Dino-Birds colliding with chandeliers, pumpkins growing down from the ceiling, their orange rinds lit up every time I breathe in and out, wreckage, treasure, old propaganda, new shipments of beliefs dumped out in the middle of a room that is actually meant for dancing. But every day I am delivered anew into a chance at making the most of it. I am your mother, and I am so good at looking at it all and saying, "Let's sort it out," over and over again, and I hardly ever tire of that pursuit. You can depend on me to help you sort things out. Remember that I am this way, that I excel at this type of task.

Your brain is becoming a mind, and my mind is trying to take itself less personally. Your body is working so hard to become appropriate for survival in this world. So much changes in both of us all of the time, and so we have to keep in touch, and keep calling it out whenever we see the changes so that we know each other as we grow, or I will think that you are the you from last week (the small person who could not sit up by herself on the quilt on the rug, but now she can). The *new* newness needs to be noted. It does not take the place of me or you from before, it only adds. I am your mother and I am a mammal with a soul that is born anew every day, and I am always arriving for you, and coming back to myself, and we will always be changing. You and I met each other during the Great Conjunction, when I had just exploded my vagina, and your lungs were broken wings, and we both got our new names.

The Stork Bite

The doctor said that the birthmark on the back of the baby's neck is called a "stork bite."

Standing there in my "pad" that was really a diaper that was cradling my own blood in a trough in my disposable underwear, and with my breasts inflated and dripping like mutant grapes from outer space, and my abdomen trampolining under my breathless, giant dress that seemed flustered or overwhelmed by what was roiling beneath it, I looked at the harmless birthmark on my brand-new baby and I felt confused because I had not been worried at all about the birthmark, and I wondered if that made me seem irresponsible or insane, and I felt that the doctor found me to be suspicious. I tried to blend in to a situation that seemed totally impossible to understand, and so I stood there like that, leaking into all of my underclothes like it was a physical state that I was at all accustomed to, and I pointed to the "stork bite" birthmark on the back of my baby's head and I said to the doctor what seemed to me to be the only thing to seriously say: "Well, Doctor, I don't know if it bit the baby, because there was a ton of commotion in the room, but I do actually think that the stork crashed into my vagina."

Letters to the Doctor: Hair Nest

Hi, Doctor—

You said, "Let me know if you have any questions," and actually I do have one. It is about postpartum hygiene and hair loss.

This morning while I was taking a shower, it was time for me to use the soap, which is the fourth out of five steps that make up the total "washing of my body process" during my shower.

The first is shampoo, the second is conditioner, the third is to brush my hair while the conditioner is in it, the fourth is to use the soap on my body, and the fifth is to let the water run down all the way from the top of the head to the ankles, until there is no more soap on me at all. I'm not sure how much you need to know? I feel like I always hear stories about people saying, "Why didn't she mention that to the doctor?" And the answer is always that it seemed embarrassing, or it seemed irrelevant, or *it seemed like it was just a pale patch of skin but then it took over her entire crotch* or *she thought it was allergies*, and for me the answer would be "She did not want to be annoying," but then you come to a point where things seem consistently off, and then after a while you just want to become well.

Right now, in my shower, my soaps are worn thin. They are still rectangles, but they have small crevices in them and they look a bit like stones washed by the sea except that they are rectangles, which is not the most natural of shapes. Have you ever found a rectangular stone on the beach, Doctor? It is almost annoying because you are like, "This is irregular and rare, so I feel pressured to keep it." And then you have your whole windowsill lined from one end to the other with rocks and fragments of glass that have been tumbled in the surf for so many rounds that they are clouded instead of clear and have no sharpness on the edges. And, Doctor, each find is like an outstretched palm, offering a confusing but activated gift, and so you take it, but the moment does not bring more. It does not "start anything" or usher in a new era because you have finally *found the amulet* that will make you into what you always knew you could be. And if you take the rock or the smoothed-down glass, and you put it on your windowsill and you accumulate a lot, people will think, "Oh okay, she's into basic whimsy. She's into blissing out and taking totems from when she was, like, *breathing deeply by the sea*." And what is hard is that even though you *did* think that the rectangular rock was "a find" of sorts, the lineup of detritus from the beach is just proof that you were stressed about *whether or not to take something,* and so you took, and then you took again, and now when you go to look out your window, you see all of this disconnected, unenchanted beach flotsam.

But re: the soaps, they are still sudsing up, so that is good news, but the fact is that I feel that at this point they all do not smell like their titular flowers, but that mostly they have the smell of the stuff they must put in the huge cauldron to cohere the soap into bars. Do you know how it used to be whale blubber? So not that, obviously, I would never use that. I am not a fucking bitch, Doctor, I would never hurt whales. But is it glycerin, maybe? Maybe it is a glycerin?

This morning I rode the thin rectangle-card of soap over my body, but especially when I would get to an area that really needs it, like armpit or butt, I would feel nervous and upset because I was not sure of what was really happening in terms of how clean I was actually getting, because I was not sure if these soaps are even soap anymore.

I would like to add that a brand-*new* bar of soap is also a problem because the edges of the brick of soap are too sharp and it can be hard to hold. It is better when the soap is in the middle of its time of being used. I wish I could apply that to myself! Like because I am in the middle of being used by life or I am in the middle of using my life? Because of my age.

The nice thing about the start of the bar is how strongly it smells, and that it can make the bathroom and even part of the hallway smell like the soap. You might walk by the bathroom and smell the lavender, and have a nice feeling of its purpleness and also have a moment of relief in which you do not feel that the bathroom presents as out of control and filthy. But of course, the bathroom does present as out of control and filthy, especially because the light fixture is filled with hundreds of dead bugs, and we are just flagrantly letting a spider live by the toothbrushes, and the wastebasket is filled with my own hair, which is rolled into little nests.

Doctor, I think there is enough background information for you now, and so I will ask my question, which is in regard to the hair I keep losing and then turning into little nests in this postpartum moment. Doctor, about the hair nests: Is there some purpose to losing this much hair and then rolling it into nests and then putting it in the trash can? I am already so stressed on my soaps and whether or not I am clean. I do not feel clean very often, no matter how much I bathe. Maybe it is the soaps? But also the act of rolling my dead hairs into nests is making me feel very unclean.

Doctor, I have already been through so much. I exploded my vagina. I ruined my knees in a weird way when my skeleton became wider over time to eventually eject the baby, and I have a dark dash of skin above my upper lip that made me say, "It's not a mustache, it's a tan" when my husband was looking at my face. And then he said that he *wasn't* looking at my face, at which point I was like, "Well, you are definitely looking at where my face *is*. My face is *right where you are looking!*" All of this, plus now a quarter of my hair will just fall out? Doctor, what is the medical purpose of this? I am fundamentally decimated already, and it feels to me like this specific work of being taken from myself, piece by piece, should be done.

Doctor, this is maybe a weird question but is some sadist-deity in the Eternal Mystery sitting on an emerald butt plug on the center of a throne made of flames and clouds, and is this sadist-deity saying, "I think we're done, but what if we do like a fun-run for a sec before we wrap, and just like, see what happens to her when we surprise her with, like, new ways to feel ugly? Guys? Eyes up for a sec? I'm about to cum, so let's firm this plan up real quick: Let's send a message to this chick, like, *You thought you knew the parameters of what defines ugliness, but you have no fucking idea, hon…* Is that bad, is that like 'hat on a hat'? I just want to see what it does. Oh, oh! Send down the thing where she is so exhausted that the exhaustion is felt as a new type of filth? But also can we go ahead and turn it inside out and make her so exhausted that she is *too tired* to bathe? And fuck with the soaps, like, make the soaps be sharp."

Doctor, is it *for* anything? I do not go on WebMD because I am afraid it will make me start to act crazy and as a woman I do not ever want to seem crazy!

I would love for you to say, "Yes. The hair of the new nursing mother falls out in a way that can simply feel mean, but this process is actually essential: There is a small, silver-feathered bird called the Phoenician Sterling Mother-bird, and she arrives at dawn to collect your hair nests. And she takes them out of the trash can in the bathroom. And, sweetheart, she takes them away so that she may lay *her* eggs on these soft circles of your fallen strands. She tends to the eggs so softly and sweetly until they hatch, and when they hatch, a *poof!* goes into the atmosphere, and it wafts *back* to the human mother who lost the hair and it goes *into* her brain, and the *poof* activates her mind again! And that is how she starts being able to have even one fucking normal thought or eventually *ideas* that are not only 'how to troubleshoot the accumulation of sludge in the drying rack for the bottle parts.' So, yes, it *is* important that your hair falls out, because if it did not, you might stay in this state where you only think things like, 'When will I ever sleep again? Read again? Stop complaining? Understand what is happening?' "

Doctor, I would like you to say, "Your instinct to gather your hairs into nests is a *wonderful* indication that this process is going as it should! Remember your all-day morning sickness and how that was actually a 'good sign'? Well, this is like that. You might think that rolling your fallen hairs into nests is a cousin to being a booger-keeper, like people who keep boogers under the flat of their school desks, but it is not. You are fine, and you are doing really well." That is what I would like you to say, but I do not expect it, Doctor.

So I guess the question really is a statement embedded in a question. What are we, at a Q&A? Ha! I used to be an actress and a writer (before when I was a person and not a *situation*), and I would go to those Q&As, and people would be told to *please ask a question* and then they would stand up, use the microphone incorrectly, and then say a statement starting with "I noticed that…" and it would just be a long statement with no interrogative in it at all. But also this is a hard memory to have because I feel very far away from these moments now because I had my baby right when the plague began, and because of the plague and also that I am now in my forties, I am not so sure that they are going to really, like, let me back in and let me do my performing. And this makes me feel furious right in my molecules, because after doing all of this, I have become so intense and able to handle so much that if I ever got to do my job in the real way that I desire to do it, I believe that I might be better than ever.

So the question that has turned into a statement is *I am very strong but extremely sensitive after having the baby.* I am proud of the way I have navigated a pregnancy and childbirth during a time of plague and disruption. But I do still feel sensitive about my body, and sometimes when the soap is too sharp, and I am already rolling my hairs into the nest in my palm, I feel jealous of the bar of soap, because it is so new and so colorful and essentially clean. And I feel jealous of my fallen-out hairs because they have finally just given up on growth! Doctor, growth honestly requires an absurd amount of patience!

So, should I switch to a medical bodywash that is for people who do not want to lose one more tiny part of themselves? Do you have that? I still use the same pharmacy, it is in your system. I would love it if you would think this over and then call in the bodywash, because I would love to start using it right away, if it is what you would recommend, of course. Thank you for your time and I hope that you enjoy the long weekend!

Au revoir!
—Jenny

A Scream

I am choosing to sit here silently but mostly because the only other thing I can think to do is a scream that ends in a question mark, which will create more work for me in the end.

Excerpt 2 from the Play *Schumacher*

LETTIE Schumacher enters the Grange Hall, accompanied by GRANDFATHER, who is her date to the Iced-Cream Social. There are many people waltzing in the hall, and the women have dance cards on their wrists, like in Meet Me in St. Louis. *Everyone is wearing old-fashioned clothes and everyone is old-fashioned. LETTIE removes her bonnet and glances at her dance card while scanning the hall, eyes traveling between couples. GRANDFATHER sees one handsome man (LUD) and a prissy-looking girl (AMANDA) dizzily waltzing, the girl giggling coquettishly. GRANDFATHER puts a hand on LETTIE's shoulder and speaks with knowing sympathy.*

GRANDFATHER:
May I offer you a glass of punch, my dear?

LETTIE:
(*Humiliated but brave*) Oh, Grandfather... Yes, please.

The young couple approaches LETTIE. AMANDA is cruel and scornful. LUD is stifling a mean laugh.

AMANDA:
Why, Lettie Schumacher! What courage you have to come here with your own grandpapa! What an absolute riot! You must have nerves of steel, musn't she, Lud?

LUD:
(*Weirdly*) Yes.

LUD seems instantly tranqed-out. He stares down, just below LETTIE's waist, to the spot where her clothing is covering her vagina. His mouth is hanging open.

AMANDA:
Lud, darling? Are you... not well?

LUD's tongue comes out of his mouth. LETTIE stands there, unaffected and pleasantly smiling as if she is watching swans in a pond. GRANDFATHER returns with a crystal glass of punch. LETTIE takes it without breaking eye contact with AMANDA.

LETTIE:
Punch! Thank you, dear Grandfather! What a splendid date you are, unlike some, I suppose? Isn't that so, Amanda? That some of the gentlemen here are a shame?

LUD is still staring, spellbound, at LETTIE's crotch area and nose-breathing in and out, super hard, like he is smelling a really good bakery smell.

AMANDA:
Lud! What on earth!?!

LETTIE sips her punch and lets her gaze drift to a large, velvet curtain across the room. There, her mother stands, also holding a glass of punch, and in the other hand she holds the velvet cord of the closed curtain, eyes trained on the clock. The hour chimes. LETTIE raises her punch glass, and MRS. SCHUMACHER raises hers, then yanks the curtain cord. The curtain rips open to reveal a gigantic window, and beyond the glass, the blinding full moon outside. The room hushes, but one violinist in the orchestra is spellbound into furiously playing one high note, so fast. AMANDA and LUD are yanked into the center of the room. MRS. SCHUMACHER brings AMANDA and LUD cocktails. LETTIE crosses to stand next to LUD; MRS. SCHUMACHER is next to AMANDA. The violinist plays, but as LETTIE and MRS. SCHUMACHER speak, the note switches from high-pitched to super low.

LETTIE:

Oh, Mama? What did you say was the name of this cocktail that we made at home in our special room?

MRS. SCHUMACHER:
Truth Serum.

LETTIE:

Do try it, Amanda and Lud! Of course, *I* don't mind if you don't, but you don't want to be rude to Mama.

MRS. SCHUMACHER raises her hand slowly, controlling their bodies like an orchestra conductor. AMANDA and LUD raise their glasses, totally possessed.

AMANDA/LUD:
(*In a trance*) Don't...be...rude...to...Mama...

LETTIE:
Cheers!

The violinist switches back to the high-pitched note as AMANDA and LUD clink their glasses with jerky movements, like windup toys. They drink it all down. AMANDA licks her lips with satisfaction and lets out an "Ahhhh" as if she's just had the most refreshing drink ever.

AMANDA:
(*Yelling like an auctioneer*) I use cruelty whenever I can! It poisons me! It is the main thing that I do! But I do not want to do this! In truth it makes me hate myself! It makes me see myself as pisssssssss!

The TOWNSPEOPLE gasp!

TOWNSPEOPLE:
Did she say "piss"?/Heavens! What kind of word is that?/It is a very dangerous word!/Amanda is ruining the party!!!

LUD rubs his tummy with satisfaction and burps crazy loud.

LUD:
Yummy yummy! I am bad, not good! I feel sad when I am bad, but still I keep being a bad little bad boy! It feels better to my body to admit that I am bad because when I lie and say that I am good, my butthole spits a bitter fog! I fog in my trousers many times a day!

The TOWNSPEOPLE scream!

TOWNSPEOPLE:
WHAT is a "butthole"?! / What kind of speaking is happening?! / Do I have a butthole? / Stand away from his trousers!

AMANDA:
(*Absolutely screaming*) I AM MEAN WHEN I HAVE MY WINE! I AM NOT IMPRESSED BY THE MORNING! I AM UPSET WHEN I AM IMPRESSED BY SOMEONE ELSE! PLEASE LET ME REPAY YOU FOR THE CRUELTIES I'VE DONE UNTO YOU, LETTIE!

CHILD:
(*Pointing at LUD's butt*) He's about to fog! Look out!

LUD farts so hard that he falls down. People scream and vomit when they catch the stench. He struggles to his knees and weeps and begs.

LUD:
Lettie Schumacher! Lettie! Please, please forgive me for the disgusting prank that I and my brothers played on you last autumn! Please forgive me for all of the wrong that I have done to you over the school years, please, Lettie Schumacher, please! Please let me pay penance!

LETTIE laughs a tiny laugh and shows no signs of stress at all. She is peaceful as she looks toward the window and at the huge moon outside.

LETTIE:

The what? Oh, Lud, darling, I hadn't given it a second thought! In fact, I thought it was quite amusing to be locked in the basement of the old church where they keep the crypts which are filled with real corpses, and especially on All Hallows Eve! Quite inventive! Wherever did you get the idea?

AMANDA:

It was my idea.

LETTIE:

Oh? Why, Amanda! What a comedian you are, my dear! Mother and I laughed and laughed and laughed, didn't we, Mama?

The violinist stops. It is dead quiet. MRS. SCHUMACHER speaks in a loud, deep, stately voice.

MRS. SCHUMACHER:

Quite amusing indeed. Quite amusing to find out that two classmates have terrorized the precious daughter that I made with my body and propelled from my loins. Quite amusing. In fact, it inspired both of us to participate in our own little larks. Come to think of it, it is quite bold of you to have somehow crawled out of that big hole that you both fell into earlier today. That hole, just a lark! So glad it didn't delay you from attending the event this evening. Now, in terms of the penance, if you'll just step to your right, Mr. Roberts? And you too, Miss Crimm?

LETTIE:
Oh, yes, be an angel and do just step to your right, Lud darling. You, too, Amanda.

Hypnotized, LUD rises from groveling and steps to the right. AMANDA shuffles over as well.

AMANDA:
I will be sorry for the rest of my life for the sorrow I caused you and your family, Lettie Schumacher.

LETTIE:
Oh? Well, Amanda, now that I think it through, I suppose it *was* rather hard on us, your perpetual cruelty in the schoolyard and your prank involving the crypt. Yes, yes, something like that is hard on the whole family. Except for Laird. He didn't care.

A huge chandelier falls on LUD and AMANDA. It bursts into purple flames. The TOWNSPEOPLE scream again!
The wreckage of the chandelier pulls in on itself, forming a tree trunk. The trunk, now purple and phosphorescent, starts growing up, up, and up. Branches extend wide and leaves sprout. The crowd

sighs and coos with wonder and delight! The tree blasts through the ceiling of the Grange Hall, branches huge and spreading farther, faster, with so much power that now the entire roof is gone. The tree sprouts Pods of all different sizes and they hang down like lanterns.

The TOWNSPEOPLE clap! In two of the largest Pods, we see the smiling, peaceful, curled-up forms of AMANDA and LUD. It looks as if they are being washed in the Pods.

LETTIE:

Ah! They made it all the way to the Pods, Mama! And once they are washed, we'll greet them anew?

MRS. SCHUMACHER:

Correct.

LETTIE:

Hmm. It took a lot of work to get it just so, but I do like it so much more than our work with the hole. It's lighter. It is prettier, and it is certainly kinder.

MRS. SCHUMACHER:

Quite right. Certainly.

LETTIE looks at the tree and the Pods. From outside the Grange Hall, the noise of an old-fashioned ambulance can be heard going by.

LETTIE:

Oh, Mama. It appears that Laird has had an accident in the bath.

MRS. SCHUMACHER:

Yes, darling, so it seems. He should have been more cautious. But then again, there are enough Pods for all of us! I'm not so foolish as to say that I myself will never need a Pod. Let's not give ourselves airs, lest we regret it.

LETTIE:

Indeed, Mama. Well put.

MRS. SCHUMACHER puts her arm around her daughter's waist and they sip their punch, mild and content as they watch their community waltz around their fine new Tree of Eternal Forgiveness.

Across the room, GRANDFATHER enjoys looking at a wall of oil paintings as he happily licks an Iced-Cream cone.

The Garbage Package

I ordered us two new mattresses because the mattress that we have was my fiancé's parents' mattress. We live in the house that they used to live in, so this is really *their* actual bed. The mattress is thirty years old at least, and I noticed that I was tensing while changing the sheets. I had to ask the empty room, "Wait, why do I live like this? I am a professional and I can buy myself a new mattress and replace the old mattress." I ordered new mattresses for our bed and the guest bedroom, and they were supposed to come yesterday, so I asked my fiancé to take our old mattress and box spring to the apartment above his store.

I started to try to write my new book yesterday, but could not bear to come and sit here and do it while the kitchen was so messy and the dishwasher was not emptied, and so I did all that. Then I came in here and wrote a psychotic piece about how every word in the book has been blessed by or given permission from the dishwasher, and I was on a bit of a roll when a huge package arrived. I thought it was the mattresses, because what makes them modern is that they come rolled up in boxes but they are mattresses.

In fact, it was a huge box of offensive garbage, some sort of "Mother's Day Gift Basket" from a Hollywood gifting company that is clearly targeting Sassy Wine Moms who love to *get real* because "Hon, that's just me." For example, the box contained a gift certificate with a card that said, "Hey Mama, take some time for you! You are a superhero!" But then the gift certificate was for a specific kind of liposuction that you can get on your arms so that you have "celebrity arms." Obviously, this is very hurtful. There was a whiskey bottle that was labeled "Foxie: Whiskey for Women," which is also weird because I have certainly always thought that all brands of whiskey are for women and I have felt fine drinking them. There were candles that smelled ass-y and herbal, and lemon-flavored popcorn, which I can guarantee nobody is hoping for. There was shampoo for people who dye their hair candy colors, and it smelled like lipstick and toxic waste. Then there were about thirty-five other bottles of shampoo. For some reason there was a very small and very stupid abstract painting, not even wrapped up but just tossed into the box, unsigned.

This is one of the worst gifts I have ever received. It is junk, it physically stinks, it all seems to do that slither-smile thing of calling you "mama" and then suggesting that you are probably cracked-up or sagging-down, and that you deserve to have someone send garbage to your house, a fake gift that you then have to dispose of. You cannot regift shampoo that smells like a Jolly Rancher merged with MRSA. I cannot pass any of these objects on to anyone I know without feeling that I am doing them dirty. Also it is a bad gift because it did not even say who it was from, so I cannot even write a thank-you note (not that I would, because I am not thankful for this, but basically it takes that option away from me, thus making me into someone who did not write a note, a rude "mama").

To make matters worse, I realized, since this was a box of garbage and not the mattresses, that we had no bed. The old bed had been taken away, and the new one had not come as promised. Our bed was now at the apartment above the store. And this box of garbage was still here and it was really huge. So then it was sitting in the middle of the entryway to our house, blocking the way to how and where I live, and a terrible thought struck me, which is that I am going to have to call my fiancé, who is already too busy at his store, and has already taken time out to take the dog to the vet today because when we touch her ear she starts crying, and I am going to have to call him and say, "Instead of the bed, a box of garbage has arrived. It seems as if I drew it to myself? You need to bring the bed back and help me throw away full bottles of shampoo and books called *How to Be as Happy as You Make Yourself Seem on Instagram*."

I am trying to write this all down, and I keep getting very tired thinking of the sociopath who invented lemon popcorn. I am getting very tired but there is no bed here and so I cannot rest, and it is all because I am strongly disgusted by old upholstery and the idea of covert fluids, and so I foolishly convinced myself that I could be taking action and living better, "because I am a professional." A professional would be doing her work right now, but this could not be "the work," right? I was hoping to write about something mystical and exquisite, yet this is all that the garbage and dishwasher have allowed.

Obituary 1

We are so fucking sad to report that the person known as (we think?) Jerry Slate has passed away during the time between dull and smart.

She was twisting in a mirror to catch a view of her back-body, and our sources report that she actually just twisted herself apart into two spirals, like molding clay from a class that they won't even give you a grade in because any impact the class might have is not valued in our power structure.

Those dancers that somehow keep staring at one spot and spin their bodies, stacked up on the corks of their toes, or those figure skaters who let the point of the blade drill them around and around in a blur on the ice, held by force but somehow also lifting a leg above their head and squeezing their vaginas shut while people judge them with scores…this was not the experience of the beloved deceased, and none of these types of people above have provided any comment here. Miss Slate spun and spun and just ripped herself in two. No blood came out. It was dead dry inside. She said a bunch of things during her lifetime, and she showed a lot too. And on the day we lost her, there she was, in the time between smart and dull, when she could still experience the faint engorgement of having a far-off idea. It is tacky, but the last pages of her diary read: *Some people make it to the top of Everest. Some people die at base camp but of diarrhea, not a hiking thing. Which one am I? Also, am I okay-looking at all anymore?*

Okay yes, yes okay, yes tomorrow when I wake up, I will try to take a peek at my butt and just see what is actually going on—I will drink at least forty ounces of water with a lime squeezed in and a pinch of salt. I eat too much sodium, and things that are fried. It's so gross. I wonder if it is okay inside my…

And then it is illegible. Ms. Slate died of supernatural or perhaps hypernatural causes, but she did not want to die, so that is really sad, actually. She is mourned by her populous indoor collection of potted red geraniums, freaked-out shit written in spilled-on notebooks, and the version of herself who was just about to arrive.

The Blessings from the Dishwasher

It is worth my time and very important to me to note that all of the words and letters used in this writing have all been blessed by the dishwasher.

It does not matter what the clock shows. It is the dishwasher who says how terrible everything would be if I were to leave her clean and full. If I were to disregard her and come here to my room to do this work, she would be loud with a screeching-gleaming, and the words that would come out would be bad. "Do me. Do me first, you know what will happen if you don't," she always says, and she is always right. I go so fast, with grace and scary speed, stacking these plates that are my mother-in-law's lovely wedding china. I am quick but careful. I am a cyclone of myself as I empty the dishwasher, returning to her open body over and over again for the plastic basket of silverware, for all of the too-many mugs that I cannot stop buying, for the little pink glass cups, for the strange low bowls that looked different in the picture on the computer.

I get it going, stacking, tucking, and my breath becomes rectangles moving in and out. There is always a moment when I could get lost in the tidying and not return here to sit down and write this archive. I could get lost because the dishwasher, feeling empty and about to be closed and left, says, "Go to the cedar closet and get the vacuum." Maybe I myself have become horny for surfaces, and I just want to wipe them all down, and hunt crumbs, and then remember the pantry, and organize the whole of it, but then I get wary about being a woman in a kitchen. Thousands and millions of years of women being trapped in the kitchen, and I think, "I should get out of the kitchen."

A sorrowful thought comes in, which is that Sylvia Plath put her head in the oven, which was in the kitchen. And so many of us were promising and very powerful, but then we ended up in the kitchen without choice or pleasure, and many were left there, abandoned in the kitchen. A kitchen can be like a friendly-seeming bog, with a sign that says, *People Have Died in Here.*

I honestly like the kitchen and I love being in there, but then I ask myself, "Yes, but why *do* you like the kitchen? For example, don't you remember in your twenties when you thought you 'liked' bikinis, but then you felt like a heartless victor over yourself when you could 'successfully' wear one? Because remember how you felt heartless because you had vanquished your *own self*? (Because you had shamed yourself into eating less so that you could look how you thought you should look in the bikini?) You experienced your win, standing high atop a grotesque mound of your own massacred self-esteem and sweetness. Remember that bikini-time? Why do you *really* like it in this kitchen?"

Well, that is definitely real. I *was* like that about my two-piece. But about me and the kitchen, it is a bit of a different story, I believe. I am not religious but it is like *Cleanliness is next to godliness,* a saying that I enjoy and use a lot. I just like to draw the words down from my mind and into a clean home. I like to feel that everything in my house knows me and that I know it and that we all help each other. So, fine, I like to clean my space. I am not a sucker anymore but I like to clean my space. And anyway, look! I am here now in the writing room. So much is coming out, it is like how you cannot hug waves when they come up on the shore. So much is being thought that I can only keep this much here on the page but there is more happening for me but I am not even quick enough to catch it.

A heavy and loud bee just came in through the window. The baby is asleep in the crib. My head is on my body and will not go in the oven because the time of my life when I was trying to annihilate myself is long over and I know it.

I am well. I am blessed by the dishwasher. She is blessed by me. We are the gods in the house and we are working in each other's image. We take turns being full and empty. We are dedicating our work to each other, we are each other's friendly inspiration. I do my work here, and I can feel in me her steely, clean, strong openness. I can feel her gathering something around the one plate in her big dark empty cube.

Letters to the Doctor: Going Crone

Dear Doctor,

I'm wondering if you have any patients or know any case studies of people in their late thirties, okay they are forty

Oops, sorry, I started sleeping all of a sudden!

I am wondering if you have any patients who are forty (or just above because they *were* in their late thirties when they started this letter but then they fell asleep and then they forgot to keep writing this for a while and now they are forty-one) who are just giving up and being old, like just skipping it all and Going Crone?

Is there a specialist you might refer me to who can help me skip over this forty-year bridge between being young-and-able-to-rebound-in-body-and-mind and old-and-gradually-stopping? If you are trying to determine whether or not I am a good candidate, please know that I often cannot see the point of exercise or getting dressed into non-soft clothes, and when I do exercise I feel that I am in real danger of irreversible injury, and when I do get dressed and wear any pants that are denim I feel pinched in my labia even if they are not high-waisted pants, and I feel pinched now, actually, and furthermore, sometimes I find myself with my forehead pushed into the cold glass of the window of the back door, thinking things like *I would actually love to quietly give up.*

Sometimes I feel that I am under surveillance for just even having a life cycle and life-form. And it feels bad, like I cannot really feel a sense of true privacy, like even when I am by myself in the bathroom there is another presence that sees my face-skin or my butt-shape and remarks flatly, "There, right there. That is where your worth is changing." I just do not like it, and sometimes I get so tired of it and so upset by the giant army of panicking people who are trying to fight the inevitable, that I say: "Okay, what are the options for just skipping this whole thing and dwelling in permissible oldness?" I feel a shameful relief when I say: "Okay, fuck it, let's Go Crone."

Doctor, please do advise, because I do not want to waste the next forty years worrying about skin wrinkles and status, worrying and being cruel toward my physical body the way I was in my twenties. I do not want to be eighty and realize that I spent forty years being a meanie and a sucker when I could have been kind and victorious on a daily basis if I'd only changed my point of view.

I sense it may be rude to Life Itself to request to skip over this bridge of time. And I guess I do admit that if I *were* to get clearance to have the treatment to go Full Crone, I might feel that I was cheating a bit. And actually I really do believe that if I allowed myself to go slowly and not turn away from anything, I might travel through my experiences feeling wonderfully connected to that which I am currently passing through.

Plus, while I was writing this letter, my husband came in and I told him what I was asking you and he said, "Why do you want to be old? Steve has Parkinson's and it's really bad." And he is right. I do not mean to be flip or glib. But I tried to explain to him that I do not want to "be old" more than I just do not love how it feels to be in this state: I feel, in many ways, younger than ever, faced with a lot of newness because of the baby, and the newness makes me feel young because I am learning something for the first time, which is something that the young often do. But I am also the most tired in my body that I have ever been, and a part of me that was there before has certainly just "stopped," and I mourn that which has been disappeared from my identity. It is simultaneous, my youngness and my oldness. It reminds me of how earth is earth, but we all know the living earth is dying, and still we all just keep living, and it is stressful and horrible to really get into the specifics of this dying, but we have to, because this is where we live.

It is courageous to carry the truth, which is that we will all get old and die, and that people will see it happen to us. So Doctor, I actually do not want to skip the bridge of time. Bridges are basically my favorite thing in architecture and definitely my favorite structures to travel on, by car or train or foot. Maybe you should start prescribing BRIDGES to people, Doctor! Ah ha ha!

I am more aware than ever that I will die.

Hopefully I will pass when I am very old. I am so glad to be alive, not just because the challenges are so fortifying, but also I am glad to be alive right now, because I know that I will also certainly die and then be dead dead dead.

Well, just disregard the start of the letter! I spent so much time writing it that I might as well mail it. Plus, I love putting stamps on envelopes and I especially love writing the return address, because it is a really satisfying reminder that I live here.

Be well!

—Dame Jenny Slate

Obituary 2

WOMAN DIES OF GOING THE EXTRA MILE

Last Friday right before serving the dinner that was not even very good and could have been a much simpler affair, the woman named Jenny Slate died of going the extra mile. Ms. Slate ended up miles and miles, and still many miles away from everyone, and she ended up in an impossible place, and it was there that she met her own mother who said THIS IS WHAT I WAS TALKING ABOUT and then she died.

Tuesday, 3:23 PM

I am feeling a feeling that lately I feel a lot at this time of day, which can only be described as *How It Looks When Someone Stares Straight Ahead but Lets Themself Tip Sideways but Totally Upright into a Pool, and They Are Wearing All of Their Clothes.*

Letters to the Doctor: A Clarification

Doctor, hey,

You may have noticed that, while I write to you a lot about really specific things regarding my postpartum/motherhood experience, I don't specifically write to you about the baby herself, nor do I write much about my fiancé (who, by the way, recently became my husband, during our wedding). It is not that they are uninteresting or tragically unmentionable. They are both essentially really great. For example, did you know that a baby never has bad breath and that you can *for real* stick your whole nose in their mouth and fully inhale and you smell nothing but basically whatever you would smell if the word "soft" came with a scent?

My baby has this type of mouth, Doctor! And call me a goblin who eats warts off of faces aka *tell me I'm gross,* but honestly, I love changing the diapers! And my husband? I like him more and more, which is notable because I already liked him so much. He does goofy dances and carries the baby in the crook of his arm like she is a bouquet of flowers.

Just in case you thought that I'd lost them but maybe you didn't want to ask me about it because perhaps you worried that the question *Did you lose your small new family?* might make me feel ashamed, I figured I should confirm that they are indeed here. But I guess it is worth saying that while one of them recently arrived into life, and one of them has had to stay strong through many changes, I am the one who was atomized, yanked into another "existential place," and who is currently drifting back together. And not to be a baby about it (although I wish I *could be,* just for the good breath that I talked about before!), but these are *my* letters to *my* doctor, so that we can have the record we need, medically speaking. So please add this information to my chart, along with this portrait that I made of me and my small new family. It's not on purpose, but the big one that looks like an ear of corn is the baby, the Christmas tree glitter sticker is my husband, and I am the spilled chocolate milk stain. As you can see I have very little talent in this medium.

Do you make any art?

Be well,
Mother/New Wife/Jenny/Wart-Gobbler
Goblin/Bad Visual Artist/Fine Clown

The Inventory

Often, when the baby is resting in the daytime, I take an inventory and I make a specific plan that would not really work for anyone else, but it helps me to feel both functional and calmed for a moment. I am happy to share my most recent inventory:

1) There are too many items hanging around because I am afraid to let them all the way go away: broken old shoes, stupid bathing suits, not cared for and very tangled costume jewelry.
2) And what the heck is going on with the socks? This is a lifelong issue.

3) Deal with it: The tiny drawers so choked with underpants that you cannot open or close the tiny drawers and you do not know what the underpants are at all.

4) The white collared shirt with the crochet? You never wear that. Put it in a box downstairs?

    4a) And do not start a weird area of "boxes downstairs" but you do not know what is in them.

5) And in the kitchen! So much will be done away with: spices that are dying into dust, a jar with no top, strange cheap shelves. Dog medicine but the dog is fine now. Some of the napkins have worried themselves into rags. How many rags do you really need? Admit that sometimes you are too guilty to get rid of a worn, ripped, or stained towel and so you say, "Put it with the rags."

    5a) Admit that you have an enormous rag collection and it is just too much.

6) There will be a box of things to save for my baby. It would be a shame if one day she is saying to someone else, "Well, my mother had this thing or that thing that would have been perfect for right now, but she tossed it away in one of her pointless fits of recalibration, one of her desperate lunges at containment and peace of mind." I hope that my daughter says what my younger sister recently said about our own mother, while our babies were playing with toys that our mother had stored for decades. She said, "She takes good care of her things." My sisters and I are our mother's things. I'll

also add that it feels really nice to show our mother how I do my own mothering and my own housekeeping.

7) I will try not to overdo it, but I *will* have to let much go. Things can lightly go away, go out easily, through a perpetual opening. But much will be saved, there will be much carefully saved for the baby: some are objects and some are actually parts of my personality that I need to keep in great condition so that she can be around them and know me as I truly am, outside of all of my tasks and what I seem like when I am trying to get them completed. When the time comes, she can decide what to do with all of it, including me, I guess. If all of this works out how I am picturing it (as I toss and store and display), she will want me to be there with her in the future when she has her own home to sort out and I am invited over quite often.

Letters to the Doctor: Purple-Dark Hole 1

Dear Doctor,

I know you said to find a specialist and that you are on vacation but please stop being on vacation and please do not send me to someone else. Doctor, if the person who is supposed to care for you actually gives up or does not want to do it anymore, and then passes it off like, "You are so messed up and un-special that you should go see a specialist for how badly you have become un-good," then I just want to say that this is not in line with "First, do no harm." It is "harm" to give up, Doctor, so for the sake of your professional legitimacy, not just for myself, but for *you,* who would lose so much if you were unable to see me through, I am going to keep being your patient.

So, basically I am definitely normal.

I have relationships. I shower and I care. I will try to eat. I think things sometimes. I function.

The issue that I am concerned with and writing to you about is the purple-dark hole marking me in the afternoons. It arrives. For example, it was there in the kitchen this afternoon. It appears right on cue, when I cannot stop myself from thinking, *I cannot believe how much time there still is before I can get into bed.* That is when it is summoned. I cannot tell if it is inside of me, or spotlighting me, or like a price tag on me, like maybe it states how much time I am costing everyone or wasting for myself.

The purple-dark hole sounds like a version of white noise that has been corrupted. Instead of doing what white noise does, which is to clean the atmosphere, to smooth it, what I hear from this hole is more of a purple noise. It is a whiny smear of a noise, and so grating. And of course this purple-dark afternoon occurrence also belches messages about me, or the state of things: *You are nothing, something bad will happen, something is bad.* And it is deeply uncomfortable because obviously I feel threatened by these statements, but I also cannot pinpoint what is bad and why I am bad or why I am nothing, yet I feel that somehow the hole is telling the truth and I should just admit it. The phrase that comes to mind and then is a perfect fit is "sneaking suspicion."

One variation within the ailment, Doctor, is that the purple-dark hole sometimes even makes me laugh! On my totally tits-to-the-wind/it's-all-over-it's-just-all-over days, it is basically that I am being haunted by a whining, floating anus! Okay, so in those moments, I allow myself an earlier than expected beer, and I laugh at the lurking, floating anus and I tell myself, "Congrats, dipshit. Some creative people are followed by colors, or snips of symphonies, or they say things like *van Gogh was really with me on those winter afternoons when I was crafting the script,* but you have somehow manifested exactly what I guess you deserve or are worth? And this is of course the whining, floating anus that is always lingering in your periphery. You cannot look it straight in the anus-face, but it can see *you* straight on, and it is all that you can produce, and it is tracking you because you are its stupid fucking mommy."

Doctor, what am I supposed to do with this? Am I supposed to fight the purple-dark hole? Am I supposed to use my very last breath to say, "No! I am not the stupid mommy of a hole. Actually, I have a *real* baby and I am a smart mother to her and she thinks I am real!"

I know what you would say. I know what would be in my "at-home care instructions": *You cannot yell at your hole, because then it makes you look crazy. And if you yell at your floating hole while you are having an early beer, you seem drunk. You would seem, to the babysitter or your husband, like you are drunk and crazy and that it was always pointless for you to ever try to do your work or be the version of yourself that you want to be.*

Am I supposed to let it eat me and turn me into some sort of underworld queen who walks this world and freaks everyone out? I cannot put myself in the hole to fill it and stop it. I have tried. It is too big, yet when I try to put myself inside the hole, I actually feel squished.

As always, Doctor, I want to "get well soon!"

I know you are on vacation and that you think I should go away, but please do not leave me, Doctor. I have come to depend on reaching out.

YOUR PATIENT,

—

Headtrip

You are on the train going away from your home, toward the city where you used to be quite young. In the past (in the city you are rolling toward in the present), you were legally an adult but only legally. You got drunk and threw up all over every sidewalk, you crashed into other tables at restaurants and shouted "Oops!," you bragged about peeing in your pants. You were in a loudly different era of your life. You were loud and this was to distract from your own inside-bellowing, knifey-young thoughts that you created but could not bear to face, like *You are small and insignificant yet your body is too big or just "wrong" and everyone hates you for this.*

You are riding the rails to the city to speak about some work you have made. You are irritated because you want to be making more work, new work, not talking about the work that was completed years ago yet is just now being shown. Even though you are traveling in service of perceived success, it honestly feels pathetic because you neither contain plans for nor hold an offer for a new job. Talking about work that you made years ago makes you feel that you *used* to be an artist, that you *used* to have the ability to create and execute ideas. Just because you are going to talk about it now doesn't mean you're still her. Chug-a-chug-a-chug, you are so hungry for new work to be given to you that you have started to panic.

How many other people on this train are currently asking themselves: *Is it a disaster?* You in the past were married to the person you made this work with, and he will be talking about it with you. It's all a bit of a resurrection, which calls attention to the fact that something died. You are attending the resurrection but you are not the thing getting to live again. This isn't the ideal attitude for going into a series of interviews. You feel the pinch of your own self-defined ineffectuality, and also the oblong pinch of gas under your left rib cage. It would be cool to just blast one right now, but you are an adult and so you are holding everything in. You have a brief blush of pleasure when you imagine being totally honest in your interviews today, not just talking about how this work is from so far away in the past, but also that you truly ripped beef on the train this morning while stressing about your career, just to add something new and relevant.

The daily confusion over whether or not you are, as they say, *always getting in your own way* is dumbfounding, similar to when people stare open-mouthed at the alien spacecraft hovering above their station wagon.

You are on the train and you think to yourself, *Well, fine then. Let me just try to restart. When I get to the city, I will cut my hair very short. Actually I will cut it all off.* This feels like an incredible remedy! And you think how good it will feel right before you let the scissors start eating, but you cannot hold that thought too well, because then you think about what you *know* will be the feeling following the first chops: You will feel doubt halfway through the shearing. You've done this to yourself before. You've convinced yourself that a haircut could solve everything. It is halfway to believing that maybe you could cut your head off and a new head would grow and think different thoughts and have higher levels of confidence and lower levels of bummer vibes.

Remember when you should have gotten divorced but instead you got a spherical haircut that also had bangs? People thought you had a perm! That was fun! But you did not have a perm. First you said, with swagger, "This is just how I look," as if you were free and had finally revealed your true self. But the ball-head had to be tended quite often, like a struggling topiary, and so while you were avoiding maintenance in your personal life, you were constantly going back to the hairdresser to do the necessary maintenance to get your ball-head reshaped. And guess what you talked about at the hairdresser? How you needed to get divorced. Eventually the upkeep was too boring, and your ball-head bounced you back to your original problem, so you finally did get divorced, but then you had to spend the next nine months of an already nightmarish era growing out an impulsive haircut.

You are on the train and you recall that the haircut wasn't just about needing to get a divorce, it was also meant to evoke hot sexiness and even a bounciness that said "Catch me, eat me!" And when you think about *that* you tell your past-self in a condescending voice, "Well, that's not very empowering, is it?" And you tell yourself, "*This* haircut I am envisioning now would be different," and "*This* haircut is about getting serious," and "*This* haircut is about quitting and disappearing and not feeling bad about that." You imagine yourself as a kind of art-nun. You have a shaved head, you have a linen tunic, you are naked under that tunic, you have one bowl, one spoon, one cup, maybe a chime that you ding instead of talking? You eat grass? That is what this haircut would be.

And even though the desire is so well developed in your mind (*I want a shorn, clean, light head*) and feels worth it to commit to, your emergency system still kicks in and shows you a really upsetting image of you growing out that shorn look, and I mean *out,* like the hairs are growing horizontally from your head, and in a puff, no curls. When you see this in your mind, you say, *Now you've really made it happen, now you look like the principal from Hebrew school,* a woman who had a dyed-brown mushroom-shaped head of puffy hair, somewhere between a cap and a pelt.

Uh-oh, that woman was one of the most disappointing adults you have ever met! Not only did she not know how to deal with crises, but when Aharon and Menachem tripped you as you were walking across the Hebrew school classroom and you went down hard and then they laughed because they meant to do it and they did it on purpose, somehow the Hebrew school principal called *you* to her office, not them. You thought she was going to give you a hug and tell you that this was not your fault, but instead she made you sit there while she called your mom and told your mom, "Yonina was wearing slippery pants and so she fell down." Your mother instantly said this was preposterous, that this is not how trousers work, and demanded to know the real truth of what happened, and this part about your mother is the only good part of this memory.

You are on the train and it is clear to you in this moment that you don't ever want to look in the mirror and see a haircut that reminds you of that woman from your past who was such a lame adult. You want to look in the mirror and be a capable adult who knows what to do when you fall down and eat shit.

You are on the train and you are pointed toward the city where, in the past, you were quite young. To the other passengers, you appear to be held in stillness. You certainly do not seem disturbed. But the real you has jumped out of your thought-abducted body, and as the train sprints itself forward, you sit in place like a stump while also running manic circles around yourself, yelling things about haircuts, art-nuns, and

Hebrew school. Nobody can see that anything is happening. Nobody can see how split up you are in yourself.

Instead of trying to stop your mind and change your head right now, you surrender and you let your mind run in circles until it is whipped into a froth of boring junk, and suddenly you do something new, which is just to sit and watch it run.

The train is getting closer to your destination. Maybe, instead of choosing a new haircut or imagining yourself as a character that you don't really want to be (art-nun), can you stay with your head rather than trying to cut it down or change it? Can you let your psyche stir itself so hard, can you face such a storm that you stir and stir in the cyclone of yourself, get hit with strange garbage that circles and circles until it becomes quieted and soft and silky? Can you stand it? Can you observe it while you do it, this risky stirring-thinking? Can you become silky in the psyche? If you can even ask yourself this, then you know there is a chance that indeed you can do it. There is a chance that you can view yourself as you spin, and this feels like it could really change a lot for you if you could know yourself as both spinner and seer.

You are on a train, which is sort of an old way to travel, but you are not old. You are on a train from the future to the place of your past, and you come bearing a message to your younger self: You are not required to bare your teeth at your own image.

You are traveling toward the city where you were young, and now you are young enough still to do all of the things that you wished for then, and you will do some of them today, when you arrive, and actually you are looking forward to it; you are proud of that work you made with your ex-husband and proud that the two of you got divorced so that you could try to be friends and artists together. Maybe you'll even say that in an interview today.

What a train ride, but you rode it out. You never closed your eyes once while it all happened on the rails just now. This whole time you have tolerated what was happening in your head. You have used your own head to tolerate what is inside of it. And actually you do not want to get away from your head—you want to use your head. And there is no time to waste, because the train is in the station and you have arrived and now you will use your head to move your body so you can get off this train and talk about what you've already accomplished.

Letters to the Doctor: Purple-Dark Hole 2

Hey, Doctor—

Not sure if you got my last one, because maybe you are not reading letters while on your vacation, but I just wanted to give you an update on the purple-dark hole that I was haunted by in the afternoons. And I am happy to say "was"!

One afternoon, I was trying to not have the beer, but I also could not stand around with the hole lurking and burping, so I thought to try lying on my side on our bed. From this position, I could not see the purple-dark hole at all. I was lying on my side on the bed and looking out our bedroom window, and I was looking at the gang of egrets by the cedars. When they are standing on the planks of the dock, they are such obvious pterodactyls that it makes me smile. I loosened a little bit, looking at the long straws of their legs and thinking about how the dinos still shudder through the forms of some of the living. And then I thought, *This is weird, but I feel that the purple-dark hole might want me to be looking at these birds, for real.*

And Doctor, looking at these egrets, I felt a sudden blast of regret! I treated this purple-dark hole as a huge annoyance, when it was only whining because it was desperate to make a request. I dug around in the issue of why I can feel so disturbed. I found an answer: It is because I feel unfinished. Not that I need to be totally complete, like a finished project, but that I feel, sometimes, these days when I "have time for myself" (but it is like two hours and I do not have the brain that one needs to have to just switch modes like that), that I have abandoned myself, that I have abandoned my own work, that I am ignoring some really meaningful requests that *I myself* am making. It does not really matter what the work is, it is that I need to be the worker. And when I am not at all the worker, not even the worker in a small way, I feel unfinished, like a house that has not been given its roof.

So, Doctor, what I am trying to get across is that I hope you enjoy your vacation, because I actually figured out the treatment for this thing. The treatment is to answer the request of the thing that is hounding me. I see now that the purple-dark hole actually *led* me to the bed, where I laid myself down and watched the egrets. They were nesting and it was natural and it would be terrible for them if they could not nest.

The purple-dark hole was not just making a request, it was gesturing at that which could help it transform. Looking at the nesting flock, I realized that I must make a nest-work around the rim of the purple-dark hole. Instead of waiting for it to leave, or kicking it out of here, I must actually surround the purple-dark hole with an overlay and underlay of the twigs and strips of my life, the ones that are receipts from requests that I *have* been able to fulfill for myself, small pieces from when my life has worked: the happiness I feel when the car windows are down and my husband is driving, the baby and how much she loves that animals have tails, or that it is great that we got the new oven, or the nature program we watched that said one time it rained for a million years straight (which is oddly soothing) or how the dog brought me a whole dead seagull as a present and it was so gross but so funny, or how for the first time in my life I'm a boat ride away from my parents and I do take a boat there, or how our house is old but I don't think it's haunted though we do have a pet cemetery with stones to mark the graves of dead dogs from eighty years ago like Cheeky and Boppy, or that I need glasses now and it was exciting to pick them out. I must gather enough of these soft, perfectly fine truths, and I must make the shape of a place for me to sit, and then sit at the center of that place the way that a bird sits in a nest. And then I believe I must wait and I can rest while I wait. I am not required to worry while I wait.

Even though, in effect, I will be sitting in the center of the nest-work, right in the middle of the purple-dark hole, I need to be clear that the nest-work is *not a toilet*. It is not like a toilet at all. I just have to say this: *Not like sitting on a toilet*. And, Doctor, I apologize for how much I said "anus" in the previous letter, although it is a medical term.

I think if I make a nest-work and settle into the center, the purple-dark hole might just rise up to make a sturdy circle-shaped cushion of natural fibers beneath me, and then it would be finished and full and no longer a hole. *It* would be a worker too, being the sturdy center. At the center would be work, weird work, but real, satisfying work. Believing this creates enough encouragement for me to begin my gathering. It is good to work these things around an emptiness until it is more of an everything, but an everything that also includes the truth of the initial emptiness. No harm, no foul, as they say, Doctor!

So anyway, I actually just want you to know that I wish you the best, and that I appreciate you. It has only been a week or so, and I don't even need to sit in the nest anymore. I move about freely but I still feel connected. Warmed by me, but now growing on its own, the purple-dark hole is beginning to seem like a bluish egg-thing, and the nest that I made is very sturdy. The egg, the nest, it is my work for sure, but I will not be able to tell you what it is until it hatches. Waiting to see what it is, that waiting is a real part of my work too, and as I said, I do not need to worry while I wait. It will be my pleasure to inform you, my treasured physician, of what has emerged.

Thanks for literally everything,
Jenny

Phase 5: Ongoing

The Swan

My father called me from the island and asked if my mother had called me from the island. Since they were both at home when he called, it was significant that he had not simply gone upstairs and asked her if she had called me. That he had not done so made me feel that he was hoping to relieve her of even one extra task, even the task of responding to him or calling me up, and so I became nervous. I said that she had not called, and then he said in a soft voice that my grandmother Connie had been having breakfast at her house, and that she had been sitting in her chair, and that she, with her head now seeming so much larger in proportion to her body (which holds her dimming life and the velveteen organs inside), slumped and fell unconscious, and that then her caregiver called the EMTs, who took her to the hospital.

My grandmother often wakes up during the night and is never mean or demanding, but begs to get dressed to see the people whom she believes have just arrived. Her house is dark downstairs, and empty of people except for her caregiver, who keeps her house spotless though the rooms are hardly used now. She begs to get dressed but it is wrong, there is nobody there and nobody on the way, because most of her friends are dead now, and it is the middle of the night. Downstairs, there is only the toaster with a few crumbs inside the apparatus, and the coffee maker which, in the late morning, will be making an amount of coffee that would be useless to me because I take enough coffee to power one of those ships that planes land on, because even though I once was her eleven-year-old granddaughter and she was a new senior citizen, we are both different now. She is a living heirloom, and I am the most physical, most mammal I have ever been because I am a new mother.

She wakes up and says that her helper does not understand that there are guests downstairs, and that she is late, and that she does not like to make people wait. She stands, string-shaped, like the formation of candle smoke when you have just blown out the candles on your cake.

My grandmother used to put her right arm out to restrain my body if she ever stopped short while driving the car. She used to say that in her next life she wanted "wash-and-wear hair," and she had an address book as long as a normal book. She is the most popular person I have ever met, and she deserves her popularity. Last summer my sisters came to swim at the pool at the place where our grandmother softly lives as a varietal of some sort of human feather. They helped her walk out to the pool that the apartments share, and in the ninety-degree heat she wore a velour tracksuit. She moved, turtle-speed yet unselfconscious, around the perimeter of the pool, saying hello to each stranger and asking them the question she has been asking at pools since the 1970s: "Would you like some grapes?" I heard about this and I felt happy that her essential birdcalls are intact. Think about yourself: If everything were stripped away, what would be your core inclinations? Would you offer strangers invisible grapes? Would you wake in the night to host a party for the dead? Would you reach your hand up to every single person's face and say thank you? She deserves her popularity.

I visited her on a different day last summer, after seeing the doctor who was caring for me because I was pregnant. I would leave the little peninsula where we live and I would drive one hour and twenty minutes to see the doctor, and this doctor would then look into my body with machines and make sure everything was fine. When I got to my grandmother's house on that day, my father was there, and he came outside and said in that same softer voice that my grandmother thought that her grandfather had died. She was not wrong, he did die, but eighty or more years ago. But still, he did die, and that is still sad.

When I came into her house, she was in a quilted floor-length peach-colored satin bathrobe that I know very well. She sat on the chair, by the telephone, looking as sorrowful and small as the last shrimp in the ocean. She was very graceful in her grief. In her life before, when her mind was still in its bowl, she had properly grieved her grandfather, and had eventually surpassed the burn of new loss. It seemed cruel to me that we patiently live through periods of anguish and shock when we lose our family members, and we keep facing it, believing that activity and time will settle it all down for us. We make a deal with fate: I'll keep this flame that signifies the one you took. I will let it scorch me in my heart if you let it die down naturally, and eventually there will just be a scar on my heart, and I will always know what I have lost. But by then, I will feel only the emptiness, not the terrible scald. I will let the fire of the loss run its course. This is the debt I will pay so that I can have a more bearable sadness.

If you were looking at us from somewhere else, looking at the humans, you would notice that there is no way for us to have our loves without breathtaking pain, not because we love brutally but because we lose each other at different times. We don't get to end together as one. You might take note of what those who remain are like when they are left on earth, conscripted into a long and terrible process of mending their hearts. If you are looking at us from somewhere else, this group of humans in mourning must be apparent, like how you see the cities with their nighttime lights when you look at us from outer space. You might see the light of the flames in all the hearts, those painful flames that go on and on for months and years.

But on that morning that I visited, it seemed that because my grandmother was dwelling in the in-between (where memories are not sorted anymore but are more like scents and smells and half-announcements), the full heat of the loss had returned and set itself once again upon our miniature matriarch, who herself had returned to her adolescent weight. It struck me as unfair. She had paid the price already. She had harbored the flame until it shrank to aloneness, until it had shrunk to the notion of "without."

I stood in front of her chair, my body triple the size of her own and containing not just me but a lifeform forming. There I was that morning, saying to her, "I'm so sorry that you're sad, Nana. I can see that you are." And then I moved the flat of my hand around the tight drum of my abdomen and showed her, "Look! I'm going to have a baby girl!" Although she could barely respond, I could see she did love that a tiny bit. She hoisted a smile from underneath her mourning. She had lost her grandfather that morning but also was gaining a great-granddaughter, it seemed. She is deeply programmed to love that type of new good news, even though of course I had told her many times already. But it was good, like getting a sick person to finally take one sip of something.

Look at us from somewhere else, like from another dimension. Look at what we do: We make our next ones inside of ourselves. Look at how we are: We hold what happened to us in a mind-bank and this is the mental-fortune that we amass, some of it horrible to keep, some of it an endless wisdom-resource. Some of it we have no idea what to do with but it must sit there in the bank.

Look at us from somewhere else, how we gather up and how we like to be around each other, how we would like to never let go. And look, from where you spy on us in your spaceship or from a god-chair in eternity: We grow so ancient. We become untethered from the dock of our reality. Look at my grandmother on that day when I stood in front of her with the start of the next iteration of our bloodline assembling in my body. With her new-old grief, she was showing me that the most tender and richest of heartbreaks (as when someone you love has died) stay down here even when you are so old that most of your mind-bank has given itself away to the deities above. Your most tender loves (and therefore your richest heartbreaks) stay with you like at the very toe of your shoe. Her sadness was like a cat at her foot, and it was with her now. I guess there is a time when the deal with fate runs out, and the mind loosens and the losses come back in bright color, and without warning, and you can say and know *my grandfather died* with as much deep, true, vascular sadness as you felt when you were young. But you are actually in your bathrobe and you are ninety-two, and now you are kind of gone but *it* is weirdly back.

My mother comes back to the island from visits to the mainland, where my grandmother lives, and she is as sad as a small girl who has lost her mother, who is not even going to be able to talk to her mother on the phone anymore. My mother is so sad about this situation that it causes other things to occur in other people, like my father not even wanting to bother her to ask her if she called me to tell me the latest news of my grandmother's increasingly free-form oldness.

My mother likes structure. She likes Shaker furniture and gardens with good-looking fences to keep out the deer. She likes pointing out old Victorian houses, she likes talking about well-placed dormers on the upper floors of houses, she likes getting stains out and restoring the fabric to its original state. She likes sturdiness, and she wants follow-through. She likes it when things have been properly restored. When I was young, she once saw her own recently dead grandmother's happy, non-scary face in the mirror she had inherited from her. My mother saw the dead, returned for a moment to affirm that she was being protected and approved.

My mother saved all of our toddler toys, and now our babies use them again, and they are in perfect condition except maybe one half of an egg has been lost from the carton of plastic eggs. That is my fault, not hers. Any irregularities are my doing. But she puts the eggs and other toys back in play because she likes to prove that things from the past still have a place and use in the present. She likes that old things can begin again in a new situation. The small loss of the half-egg is a part of how we all play. We cannot fix the loss. We try to go with it.

Three years ago my mother's best friend died. Before that, they would talk on the phone every day. Before her best friend died, she told my mother that she would come back as a swan and drift around on the little pond off of one of the main roads on the island. Like a child, but also like a heart-strong adult, my mother believes in the absolute request placed in this mysticism, and when we drive past the pond, she comments plainly on the fact that her friend has not yet returned to her. It is said in the same tone as "The restaurant has a new chef and now it is not as good."

A year after my grandmother experienced the renewed death of her own grandfather, my father told me over the phone that my grandmother did slump and sleep at breakfast, but she did not die right then. She *is* dimming into death but it is a relief that she is not in pain, good that she is not ever mean or agitated, and is being rocked and rocked slowly into the next level. As she is cradled by the swaying of her gentle departure, she experiences waves of her life from before. Some are her heartbreaks, some are her achievements and greatest qualities, like being a wonderful host, like being able to be so happy by the sight of a new life.

When I bring my daughter to her, my child seems to view my grandmother as a big fancy, gentle bird. My daughter is not afraid to touch her taloned hands. She is inclined to sup with her great-grandmother. They sip soup together, two beings with caretakers who make sure that they stay clean and can get the food into their mouths.

My grandmother used to participate in synchronized swimming, went to Gail's Beauty Parlor once a week for more than fifty years, sang Hebrew prayers dutifully and in a tone-deaf voice and with a Boston accent, and had "Keep Abortion Legal" stickers on her kitchen cabinets. One time while my sisters and I sat up in her bed, dressed in her nightgowns and jewelry, she reenacted the moment my grandfather proposed to her, and she was wearing her bra and slip when she did this performance for me and my sisters, and she was sixty-five years old then, and I remember thinking that she was the prettiest person that I had ever seen.

If you look at us from another world, from another planet, from the point of view of another species, it must seem psychedelic and excessive, how many times we transform over our lifetimes.

My mother is taking this the hardest—it is too much of a loss, this final, remote form in which she finds her sweet mother, whom she needs to be real and last forever. I want to be right next to her on the day that my grandmother's body rests and the other parts travel elsewhere. I, like my father, am a bit frightened that my mother will be totally incinerated by the flame of the loss. She is having a hard time loosening her grip on what needs to go, and friction makes the flame, does it not?

I cannot be a mother to my mother. I am having a hard time cutting a deal on this one. Of course I know there is not one to be had. But I do hope that when my grandmother leaves us, my mother will be flush with memories of what my grandmother was for so long, and not just overtaken by images of how she broke down at the end. I hope that these memories will be the dominant ones, that they will be more precious than ever, and perfectly restored for her. I hope that I will be with her in the moment when she is soothed by the concept of mystical sturdiness, of follow-through, of restoration.

I hope I will be with her and my daughter in the car, driving past the pond on the island, and that I will look out and be the one to tell her, "Look there, the swan has finally arrived." And when the swan is on the pond, we will know that the other beloved are soon to make a spectacular return.

Lettie Schumacher Memorial Plaque

This plaque marks the spot where Lettie Schumacher (1886–2020), beloved Community Enchantress, ascended from earthly life. Just before her ascendance, she manifested as old, glowing purple bones enrobed in early-1900s-style evening wear made out of swaths of honest light. Fearsome and exacting in her youth, Lettie developed what we now know as "Emotional Sorcery," an ancient Druid discipline, taught to her by her mother, Ogma, who was an ancient Druid of uncountable age. Many noted that at the start of her tenure as the first and only Community Enchantress, there was much gore and disruption, but, as Schumacher explained in her first public conference, which she held while hovering over Farmer Randall's gorgeous summer bathing pond, *"This initial burst of punishment and power will not touch anyone but those of the living who are currently being total tools. And even those souls who are struck down in this season of recalibration for our community will be absorbed into the Tree of Eternal Forgiveness (located in the multipurpose room of the Grange Hall) so that they may be properly washed and warmed in a Pod until they are suitable to return. It is only terrifying now because all of the small and large degradations and abominations are being made to surface, like when the dead trout float on their sides in the pond and make a stink. But soon our world will be whole and scented and silky. Thank you to my mother for passing on this knowledge that I have developed, and to Farmer Randall for welcoming us all at his pond and lovely fields today."* Lettie Schumacher guided the community for 134 years, until she felt the glimmer of "newer work" and "further development," at which point she gathered the people on this spot, gulped in huge portions of light until she became a Moon, bounced like a ball through the assembly, and ascended into the face of the setting Sun. She named no successor because she believed that it could have been anyone.

The Graduation Speech

Hello and thank you for inviting me to speak today, and congratulations to all of this year's graduates.

Class of 20[—]: I am not saying that people are *making* me have yogurt.

I do not feel pressured to purchase it, or that I need to eat it because of something that is making demands on me about yogurt. So, this is not a complaint about yogurt. What I want to speak about today is how to be resourceful in creating new options for experience. And yogurt is a part of that for me.

When I have yogurt, I like to pretend that it is a custard made for me by a small enclave of elves, like a ceremonial custard made for an honored guest who is visiting from afar. I think about the elves choosing which fruits with which to flavor the custard, and that the cream for it is poured from a lovely pitcher, by the mini hands of an elf. I think of the expert stirring done by an older elf, with a wooden spoon that *that* elf got from an *even older* elf in the family. I see it all from above, the spoon making the circle in the thickening cream and sugar. I like thinking of the elves describing this dish in their cultural books, calling it "a very special custard, served cold." I say to myself that they have a name for it, like "Wanderer's Pudding."

I put it in a small glass bowl, and of course I eat it slowly with a small spoon, and I act like they are watching me, hoping that I am loving it, and I am. I am loving it.

This is a luxury that costs but the price of a common yogurt, and the thrill does not wear away.

This is one example of an acceptable way to have a secret thing that you do, and to really feel that thrill of "Nobody knows that I am doing this thing that I am doing right here." This yogurt-thing is a secret thing to do but is not "bad," and there is no lying involved, but you are still fooling people a bit and it is fine, and well within the margins of kindness.

The only ones who would not be fooled are the elves.

It can be a bit lonely to know of this wonderful way to live your life. There is the feeling, at times, that if you actually did tell anyone that you were doing what you were doing, they might think that you are "out of it" and not in control of yourself, when in fact you are in great control, which is why you are able to take a boring experience like *eating yogurt at the table* and do the refreshing work of letting yourself feel that you are an honored guest spooning out a ceremonial custard, and experiencing the kindnesses of enchanted beings who hope that you are always comfortable.

The potential for loneliness to occur is a price, and yet you might find that having yogurt this way is worth it. And you will feel sure that others might love it if they too could try it, but many will not ever care to try, and many will turn away from you because they are afraid of what it would feel like to feel "silly" for even one minute. A lot of people simply will not understand you, which will feel like an unsettling warping, which I am feeling right now.

But I am still able to continue speaking and I am still the official speaker at this graduation.

That said, I do not feel that I am the appropriate person to give you advice, because I am not interested in that. I do love to tell people about how I have found ways to create daily enchantments for myself. Every time I tell about what I do, and I lay out how I do it, I feel that I reconfirm my mindset. So, thank you for letting me be here.

I suppose if there were something valuable that I could leave you with, it would be to say that you can play tiny invisible games inside of your plainest tasks, and that this changes the truth of how you are in your world.

Honored graduates, I am not a goofing, foolish kook. I am a serious person, in my way. I am inclined to be happy, and also stormy and sad. It has helped me along to play small games of pretend, even as I am in the most stony circumstances. It has cost me nothing, kept me sane, kept me open and young, and is the one way that I have found I can keep a cozy light on when I experience my existence as a darkened homestead.

I hope that you will be thoughtful about making your experiences. To be thoughtful about what you want to be feeling, and to invent roads to get there, are two of the loveliest ways toward empowerment and satisfaction. My wish for all of you is that even the biggest grumps and total duds among you today find one moment in the next seventy or so years to pretend that you are on the receiving end of a ceremonial pudding.

Thank you for this honor, congratulations on it all. I wish you all a pleasant summer, and much comfort in your long lives.

Prayer: Fountain

O dear infinity-number of deities, please do not let me be the master of the regretful smile.

Please do not ever let me be the compulsive sidearm flinger of the involuntary scoff.

Let me be the clean-mouthed laugher with tears running down the cheeks, and make it be that I am only weeping because I am too full of and spouting a syrup from surrendering to sweetness.

Make it be that I am the fountain of it. I will work hard to remember that I am not required to be in combat anymore, and that I am doing the silky work of forgiveness now. Let me live like this, and when I die, mark my place with a fountain that feels encouraging to look upon. Don't even write what my name was. Do not mark my dead bones, just build the fountain there as something that everyone feels invited to enjoy, and even if hundreds of years go by and the fountain falls apart and is nothing but stones in a field, make it that travelers look upon the ruin and taste a ghostly trickle of sweetness. Stand that fountain up over my buried bones, put it there as a sign of what I hoped for while I was briefly here.

Acknowledgments

Thank you to my editor, Jean Garnett, a brave, persistent, thoughtful, funny, brilliant person who worked with me, listened to me, and is astoundingly generous with her time, brainpower, and incredible skill. Thank you to the early readers who read drafts and rewrites and talked with me a lot about this work: Elisabeth Holm, Todd Oldham, Deborah Kovacs, Gabe Liedman, Daniel Zomparelli, and of course my wonderful agent Claudia Ballard, as well as my representatives Josh Pearl, Shauna Perlman, and Stacy O'Neil. Thank you to my dear friend Rebecca Dinerstein Knight, the central reader who gave me great hope and peace of mind during this process as she sifted through it all with the magical diligence and enchanting intelligence that only she possesses. Thank you to my father, Ron Slate, for reading and reading and reading it, for his continued support of me as a writer and person, for letting me park myself on the couch for a week so I could ask him what he thinks. To my sisters, Abby Ciampa and Stacey Slate; to my best friend, Quinn Lundberg: thank you for holding me up, for keeping me very safe. Thank you to Max Silvestri, Leah Beckmann, Lang Fisher, Gillian Robespierre, Rachel Antonoff, Steph Jenkins, Jon Low, Zach Galifianakis, Ed Helms, Sarah Bastian, Mike Ciampa, Cindy Ko, Will Shattuck, and Bill Shattuck for your friendship and love. Pamela, thank you for your support and insight. Thank you to Chayla Wolfberg and Karen Garner for being so sweet and helping me keep everything straight in my life so I can actually get to work. Thank you to the people who have watched my daughter and cared for her so I could accomplish this dream of writing another book: Trish Gardner, Dante Bates, Darian Lopez Ciarelli, and especially Jen White, a gift of a person who not only cares for our daughter while my husband and I do our work, but also offers me such abundant support (especially when I was a new and nervous mother). And a huge debt of gratitude to my mother-in-law, Dedee Shattuck, who (for months) arrived smiling, breezing through the kitchen door every day at 6:30 AM so I could do some early-morning writing. Thank you to my daughter, Ida, for making my heart into a superconductor, for finding me in this dimension, for joining me in love and in the unknown! Thank you to my husband, Ben Shattuck, for so much childcare and encouragement when I go to work, and so much care for me when I return, for partnering with me in romance and life, and for being such a consistently fun, honest, and sweet person who is strong enough to be open and invested in growth. How could I have even *met you?* Let alone *marry you?* It's too much. Thank you, Ben and Ida, for existing. Thank you to Nanas Connie and Rochelle, and to my grandfathers, Paul and Lester. And to my mother, Nancy Slate, thank you for *everything.* Through my own parent-eyes, I see you in the past, and now I see many things that I never saw before. So, for everything, for then, for now, forever, thank you, Mom. You gave me my heart.

About the Author

Jenny Slate is an actor and stand-up comedian and the author of the essay collection *Little Weirds* (an instant *New York Times* bestseller), as well as the *New York Times* bestselling children's book *Marcel the Shell with Shoes On*. Her feature film *Marcel the Shell with Shoes On* (which she cowrote and starred in) has been nominated for many awards, including a Critics' Choice, a Golden Globe, and an Academy Award. Jenny Slate lives in Massachusetts with her husband, Ben; their daughter, Ida; and a great dog named Sally. She is a graduate of Columbia University.